WANAKA

LAKE, MOUNTAIN, ADVENTURE

Neville Peat

Otago University Press

Published by Otago University Press
Level 1, 398 Cumberland Street
Dunedin, New Zealand
university.press@otago.ac.nz
www.otago.ac.nz/press

First published 2002
This revised and redesigned edition published 2018
Copyright © Neville Peat
The moral rights of the author have been asserted

ISBN 978-1-98-853136-6

Editor: Imogen Coxhead
Index: Anna Corballis Fry
Maps: Allan J. Kynaston

Front cover: Lake Wanaka from Roys Peak, with the islands
of Mou Tapu and Mou Waho prominent beyond Roys
Peninsula. ROB BROWN WWW.ROBBROWN.CO.NZ
Title page: Roys Bay foreshore
Back cover: Yachts on Lake Wanaka
'High Country Weather' by James K. Baxter on page 22:
copyright © The James K. Baxter Trust. Source: *James
K. Baxter Poems*, Selected and introduced by Sam Hunt
(Auckland University Press, 2009)

Printed in China through Asia Pacific Offset

CONTENTS

ACKNOWLEDGEMENTS   4

Information centres 4 • Local distances 4 • Map 5

1. A PLACE IN THE SUN   6

That Wanaka tree 8 • Oanaka: An ancient crossroads 14 •
European history 16 • The lakes 20 • Weather word 22

2. TOWN AND AROUND   24

Events calendar 27 • Year-round attractions 30 • Camping 32 • Drives 34

3. A REGION MADE FOR WALKING AND CYCLING   38

Map 40 • Town walks 42 • Longer tracks 45 •
Makarora walks 52 • Cycling 53 • Climbing 54

4. WATER AIR AND SNOW   56

On the water 57 • Wanaka's islands 58 • Going fishing 61 •
In the air 62 • On the snow slopes 64

5. THE WILD SIDE   66

Bird life 67 • Plant life 73 • Lizards 75 • Wētā 75 •
Mount Aspiring National Park 76

INDEX   78

ACKNOWLEDGEMENTS

I am grateful to the following for advice and information: James Helmore, Callum MacLeod, John Darby, Annette Grieve, Sonya Sawyers, Desiree Whitaker and Gilbert Van Reenen. Unless otherwise acknowledged, photographs are by Neville Peat. For images and photographic assistance, thanks to Rob Brown, Lee Eadie, Chris Riley, John Darby, Margaret and Ken Thomlinson (Upper Clutha Historical Records Society, UCHRS), Stuart Thorne, Sophora Peat, Ian Southey, Nadia Ellis, Nicola King, Mandy Deans, Stephen Thompson, Jeno Hezinger, Tess Hellebrekers, Ian Turnbull, Gregor Richardson and Stephen Jaquiery.

INFORMATION CENTRES

Wanaka
Lake Wanaka Information Centre (iSite)
103 Ardmore Street
Phone: 03 443 1233
Email: bookings@wanaka.co.nz
www.lakewanaka.co.nz/visitor-centre/

Tititea/Mount Aspiring National Park Visitor Centre
Ardmore Street
Phone: 03 443 7660
Email: mtaspiringvc@doc.govt.nz
www.doc.govt.nz

Lake Wanaka Tourism
www.lakewanaka.co.nz

Makarora
Department of Conservation office
www.doc.govt.nz

HOW FAR FROM DOWNTOWN WANAKA?

Albert Town 5km
Alexandra 86km
Cardrona 25km
Christchurch 427km
Cromwell 55km
Dunedin 272km
Fox Glacier 260km
Glendhu Bay 12km
Haast 145km
Invercargill 242km
Lake Hawea 15km
Makarora 64km
Mount Cook 208km
Omarama 113km
Queenstown 67km via Crown Range;
　　117km via Cromwell
Waterfall Creek 3km

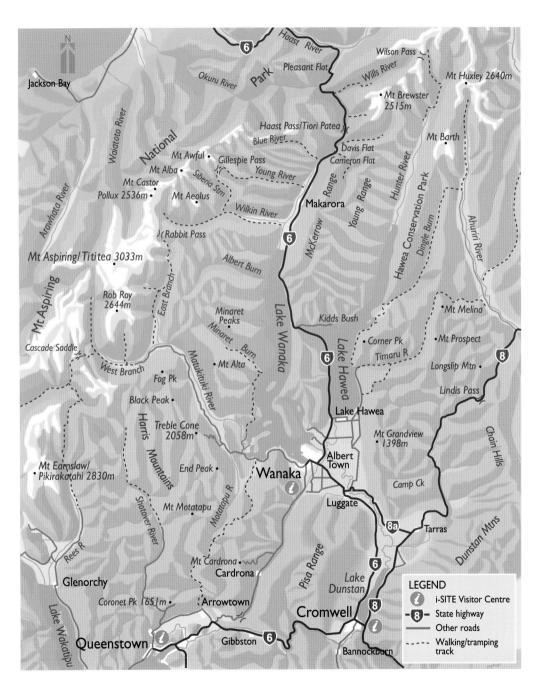

N

Jackson Bay

Haast River

6

Wilson Pass

Pleasant Flat

Wills River

Mt Huxley 2640m

Okuru River

Park

Mt Brewster
2515m

Waiatoto River

National

Haast Pass/Tiori Patea

Mt Barth

Blue River

Davis Flat

Mt Awful

Gillespie Pass

Cameron Flat

Mt Alba

Siberia Stm

Young River

Mt Castor

Pollux 2536m

Mt Aeolus

Wilkin River

Makarora

Arawhata River

McKerrow Range

Young Range

Hunter River

Hawea Conservation Park

Dingle Burn

Ahuriri River

Rabbit Pass

6

Mt Aspiring/Tititea 3033m

Albert Burn

Mt Aspiring

Rob Roy
2644m

East Branch

Minaret
Peaks

Minaret Burn

Kidds Bush

Mt Melina

Lake Wanaka

Corner Pk

Mt Prospect

Cascade Saddle

West Branch

Mt Alta

6

Timaru R

Longslip Mtn

8

Fog Pk

Matukituki River

Lindis Pass

Black Peak

Lake Hawea

Harris

Treble Cone
2058m

Lake Hawea

Mt Grandview
1398m

Chain Hills

Mountains

End Peak

Albert
Town

Mt Earnslaw/
Pikirakatahi 2830m

Wanaka

i

Camp Ck

Shotover River

Mt Motatapu

Motatapu R

Luggate

Rees R

8a

Tarras

Dunstan Mtns

Mt Cardrona

Pisa Range

Glenorchy

Cardrona

Lake
Dunstan

6

Coronet Pk 1651m

Arrowtown

8

Lake Wakatipu

Queenstown

i

Gibbston

6

Cromwell

8

i

Bannockburn

LEGEND

i — i-SITE Visitor Centre

8 — State highway

—— Other roads

- - - - Walking/tramping
track

1

A PLACE IN THE SUN

THE WANAKA REGION covers a 6000 sq km block of western Otago, with Lake Wanaka at its centre. It ranges from Makarora in the north to Cardrona in the south. Lindis Pass marks the eastern boundary, and the western side encompasses Tititea/Mt Aspiring and the Skippers area. Lakes Wanaka and Hawea, and the Upper Clutha, Hawea, Cardrona and Matukituki rivers, are the main water features. Much of the region is filled with mountain ranges, including a section of the Southern Alps in the northwest corner, the Harris Mountains west of the Matukituki Valley, and the Pisa and Criffel ranges south of Lake Wanaka.

Wanaka can thank the ice ages for its lake and mountain setting, its extraordinary scenery, its sunny spaciousness. The town is anchored on a ridge of rock debris dumped by a retreating glacier. Lake Wanaka was created by the damming effect of that terminal moraine and by successive glaciers grinding and scooping out a bed to depths below sea level. Glacial ice also smoothed the sides of the valleys in the region, spilling down the Matukituki and Makarora valleys and eventually joining with the Hawea Glacier to extend down the Clutha Valley almost as far as Cromwell. The result of all this primeval shapeshifting is a spectacular landscape.

The last glaciation (in two million years of ice ages) peaked about 18,000 years ago,

LEFT: River, lake, mountain, sky … afternoon autumn light brings out the colours in this view from the summit of Rocky Mount near Lake Diamond, a popular destination for day trampers. Lying off the braided mouth of the Matukituki River is the wooded island of Mou Tapu.
RIGHT: Poplars gild the western shores of Roys Bay in autumn.

THAT WANAKA TREE

Whoever dug a willow fencepost into the edge of Lake Wanaka at the western end of Roys Bay some 80 years ago probably never imagined the post growing into a tree, let alone the tree achieving international stardom in the new millennium. As willows go it is unassuming, lopsided and somewhat stunted for its age, but its beautiful setting – a skirt of glacial lakewater and a jagged section of the Southern Alps as a backdrop – is what makes it a star attraction.

In 2014 another kind of post – #thatwanakatree on Instagram – launched the lonesome, winsome willow as a highly sought-after photo location. The tree became a social media sensation, and since then people of all nationalities, including newly-weds and the occasional nudist, gather at all hours of the day and night armed with selfie-sticks in search of the perfect photo opportunity.

That willow is almost certainly New Zealand's most photographed tree. Ironically, the crack willow *Salix fragilis* – also known as brittle willow – is an introduced species that can spread along waterways and damage native habitats, including those that draw international visitors to New Zealand in the first place.

TOP: Sunrise over Roys Bay on a chilly July morning. ABOVE: A crisscross pattern of lines on the mountains near the Neck, opposite the Kidds Bush area. The lines angling right to left are likely to be caused by fractures or joints in the rock.

and the ice began retreating rapidly 10,000 years ago – just a blink in geological time. Wanaka, on the eastern edge of the Southern Alps, is enjoying a breather from the ice, a time in the sun.

The town centre looks west to snowy peaks that hint of colder times. The mountain fastness, ragged-topped, is close enough to feel powerful but not threatening or claustrophobic. Between the town and tall mountains, the lake has a gleaming, softening presence. The proportions are just right. There is a serene coherence to it all.

That this agreeable mix of mountains and water attracts visitors is no recent thing. Wanaka's first substantial building was a hotel, established in 1867 by Theodore Russell. He recognised the tourism potential, especially for sightseeing on the lake. Before long, steamers were regularly carrying visitors to the islands and all the way to the top of the lake, the Makarora end. Recreational deer hunting, with massive trophy heads the drawcard, added to the appeal of Wanaka. Tourism carried on into the early twentieth century, with ladies in lace and long dresses and well-dressed gentlemen enjoying lake cruises and short walks to scenic delights, such as Arethusa Pool on Harwich Island, now named Mou Waho.

Through the mid-twentieth century Wanaka remained a summer holiday destination, especially for Dunedin people, but compared to other lakeland resort areas – notably Queenstown – it had a backwater feel to it. It was a relatively quiet spot located somewhere between the dry interior of Otago and the lofty wet mountains away out west. Wanaka township, in the 1950s, had all the appearance of a sleepy farm-service centre.

The road to the West Coast via Haast Pass, opened in 1960, changed Wanaka's status. As more and more of the road became tarsealed, the town benefited from the traffic flowing to and from the glacier tourist towns on the coast. The opening of Mount Aspiring National Park in 1964 also put Wanaka firmly on the map. The national park headquarters were located in the town, and the area became a marshalling point for countless trampers, climbers and sightseers.

Following the development of a number of skifields, since the 1980s there have been breathtaking changes. Wanaka is now a year-round landmark destination with multiple roles: with a calendar of highly popular events, it is a mecca for summer and winter outdoor pursuits, a retirement town, a backpacker base, a farm-service centre, and the gateway to Mount Aspiring National Park and the southern West Coast. It is a compelling stop for tourists exploring the South Island and, judging by the sprawling subdivisions and elaborate architecture, ranks as a playground for the wealthy.

TOP: Visitors feeding birds from the town jetty.
ABOVE: The Wanaka Marina in Roys Bay.

Winter sunrise over Roys Bay, the Buchanan Peaks and Mt Alta.

Each five-yearly census in recent times has confirmed Wanaka's boom status. The population is expanding rapidly: the 2013 census recorded 6500 inhabitants, and projections for 2018 indicate this may have grown to over 8000. Wanaka's housing stock is increasing at a commensurate rate: 4500 dwellings were recorded in 2013, of which around 40 per cent were unoccupied holiday homes, and since then many subdivisions have proliferated on the town's fringes. Nearby, Lake Hawea's population and dwelling counts reflect a similar but smaller trend.

Comparisons with Queenstown, about an hour's drive away via the Cardrona Valley, are inevitable. Both towns lie within the Otago region but Queenstown has strong links with Southland. Both make the most of their lake and mountain settings, but where Queenstown lies in a geological and climatic transition zone between Central Otago and Fiordland, Wanaka is firmly on the edge of Central Otago, and its climate and landforms are typical of Central.

As the twenty-first century unfolds, suburbia Wanaka-style is stretching northwards to Albert Town on the banks of the Clutha River/Mata-Au and westwards towards the Cardrona Valley. The commercial/semi-industrial zone has expanded and more schools and other facilities are under construction. Wanaka's retail and business centre occupies just a few blocks, a remarkably small area given that it has to handle visitor volumes of around 1.5 million a year. The district council and local community board are hard-pressed to manage the stresses on infrastructure that are the result of ever-increasing numbers of residents and visitors.

The town's tourism industry is said to generate over $500 million a year, with Lake Wanaka

ABOVE: Edgewater Resort's attractive grounds overlook Roys Bay adjacent to a lakeside walkway and cycleway. BELOW RIGHT: Self-contained campervans crowd the town centre. BOTTOM: Russell lupins flower profusely in summer near Beacon Point.

Tourism reporting 470 tourism operations of one kind or another in 2018. Wanaka has achieved 10-year tourism goals in just four years, but that kind of growth comes at a price. For example, the lakefront at the head of Roys Bay – perhaps the town's primary scenic attraction – is frequently beset by camper vans and other vehicles, and traffic backs up at the roundabouts. Plans to ease the pressure include the creation of a vehicle-free lake edge in front of the business area and Pembroke Park, as well as the redirection of traffic around the town centre.

Wanaka is in the process of reinventing itself. As long as development retains a sense of proportion, is fit for purpose and does not compromise natural values, Wanaka will continue to be a place where you can commune with the mountains, watch the weather change, savour the sunsets and marvel at the clarity and entrancing quality of the light. There will still be a place in the sun.

TOP: Towards Christmas, native mistletoe flowers appear in beech forest at Kidds Bush, Lake Hawea. ABOVE: Kōwhai trees flower in spring.

OANAKA: AN ANCIENT CROSSROADS

Wanaka was an area of strategic importance for pre-European inhabitants. The name 'Wanaka' has sometimes been interpreted as the southern version of 'wānanga', which refers to ancient Māori schools of learning. The area's alternative name, 'Oanaka', is said to describe a crossroads or meeting place, and traditional trails certainly passed through the area. Parties travelled inland from the East Coast on a seasonal basis in search of food, fibre and stone. Food was plentiful in this landscape: eels/tuna and birds – moa, weka, grey duck/pārera, pigeon/kererū, quail/koreke, kākāpō and others – were abundant, and plant foods such as cabbage tree/tī kōuka stems and bracken fern root or aruhe could be gathered. Lakes Wanaka and Hawea were both renowned for their eel fisheries, and the fish were caught in great quantities, preserved and transported back to coastal settlements.

In pre-European times there were various Māori seasonal campsites around the lakes. These included Takikarara near where the town of Wanaka now stands, Nehenehe in the lower Matukituki Valley, and Manuhaea on the Lake Hawea side of the Neck near the road to Kidds Bush. The Takikarara settlement was renowned for its whare wānanga or school of learning.

Southern Māori traditions tell of the explorations of the legendary Rākaihautū in the waka (canoe) *Uruao*, who travelled down the South Island from Nelson on an inland route carrying a digging stick or kō that had magical powers. It was Rākaihautū who dug the beds for the great southern lakes and made the region habitable for the people who came after him.

The name Hawea is thought to commemorate an ancestor, Hāwea, who led the Ngāti Hāwea hapū (subtribe) of the southern Waitaha people.

SIGNIFICANT PEAKS IN THE WANAKA REGION

Tititea/Mt Aspiring 3033m
Mt Alta 2339m
Black Peak 2289m
Treble Cone 2058m
Roys Peak 1581m
Mt Iron 750m

TOP: Ironside Hill on the Millennium Track west of Waterfall Creek.
ABOVE: West Matukituki River, with Mt Ansted (2388m) in the distance.

EUROPEAN HISTORY

Grass and gold figure largely in the European history of Wanaka region. Grass was the first attraction. Vast areas of native tussock grassland were set aside by the provincial government for sheep farming in the late 1850s, following an epic journey of exploration and surveying through the Otago interior in 1857 by the province's chief surveyor, John Turnbull Thomson.

Wanaka Station was established in 1858 and stretched from the Cardrona Valley to the head of Lake Wanaka. It carried up to 100,000 sheep, mostly merino. Initially based at Albert Town, Wanaka Station homestead was moved to Roys Bay in 1913. The site was later gifted to the people of the district as Wanaka Station Park, a pleasant woodland area beside the lake at the western end of Pembroke Park.

Glendhu Bay about 1910. A.H. MCLAREN PHOTO ALBUM, UCHRS

OPPOSITE, TOP LEFT: Pembroke, 1906. The house at left still stands in McDougall Street, with large sequoia trees towering above it today. The western side of Roys Bay was predominantly farmland in the early 20th century. BURTON BROS/HOCKEN COLLECTIONS

TOP RIGHT: Farming heritage – merino ewes and lambs near Lake Hawea.

BOTTOM: The Clutha River near Albert Town, with the Criffel Range in the distance.

During the 1860s, following a curtain-raising goldrush near the Lindis road, some 3000 gold miners poured into the Cardrona Valley to work the diggings on the Criffel Range and the valley floor. The Otago goldfields created a huge demand for timber, and much of this was sourced from native forests in the Makarora and Matukituki valleys. Logs and timber from local mills were rafted across Lake Wanaka and down the Clutha River to Albert Town, which was the district's main centre during the goldrush years. Travellers – and Wanaka Station's sheep – were ferried across the river at this point.

Pembroke from above Lakeside Road. ALEXANDER MILNE COLLECTION, UCHRS

Wanaka in the 1930s. Wanaka Hotel, built in 1923, burnt down in 1958. ALEXANDER MILNE COLLECTION, UCHRS

A calm evening at the Chalmers Street lookout.

In the 1880s, as tourism on Lake Wanaka grew in popularity, Albert Town relinquished its role as main town of the district to Wanaka, then called Pembroke after a British colonial secretary. On 1 September 1940 the town was officially renamed Wanaka.

The first European to set foot in the Wanaka region was Nathanael Chalmers, an adventurer and farmer who, in 1853 at the age of 22, made a three-week round trip inland from Southland with two Māori guides. At Lake Hawea Chalmers insisted he was 'too fagged to proceed further'. His guides then made a raft of raupō stems for a speedy return journey down the Clutha River to the coast.

The first known painting of Lake Wanaka was completed by surveyor John Turnbull Thomson in December 1857. From somewhere near the top of Grandview Mountain, east of Hawea Flat, he painted a watercolour image showing Roys Bay and Stevensons Arm, the Clutha and Hawea rivers, Mt Iron, and a backdrop of sharp, white mountains. In his fieldbook he noted:

> At the head of Hawea, distance about 40 miles [64km], is a very lofty snowclad peak which I called Mt. Aspiring.

Tititea/Mt Aspiring (3033m) is certainly the highest mountain in the Wanaka region, and the highest outside Aoraki/Mount Cook National Park, but from the summit of Grandview Mountain it is largely obscured. Modern research concludes that Thomson's 'snowclad peak' was more likely Mt Aeolus (2283m), formerly known as Oblong Peak, which lies further to the north. The name Mt Aeolus was applied in 1985.

Cabbage tree (tī kōuka) flowering at Timaru Creek near Lake Hawea.

LAKE WANAKA

Altitude 277m
Surface area 192 sq km
Length 45km
Maximum width 11.6km
Maximum depth 311m
Catchment area 2590 sq km

LAKE HAWEA

Altitude 338–346m
Surface area 138 sq km
Length 42km
Maximum width 13.5km
Maximum depth 393m
Catchment area 1394 sq km

THE LAKES

Wanaka and Hawea are glacial lakes that together form a major part of the Clutha catchment. They are separated by a narrow saddle known as the Neck, which you negotiate on the highway between Wanaka and Makarora. Lakewater temperatures normally range from 9 to 10°C, while the rivers feeding the lakes range from 8 to 9°C.

Wanaka is New Zealand's fourth-largest lake after Taupo, Te Anau and Wakatipu. The outlet of Lake Wanaka marks the start of the Clutha River/Mata-Au, New Zealand's largest river by volume. Big from the outset, it averages 200 cubic metres per second (representing 35 per cent of the river's mean flow of 560 cumecs at the mouth near Balclutha).

Lake Hawea is controlled by a dam that stores water for hydro-electricity plants on the Clutha River at Clyde and Roxburgh. Completed in 1958, the dam raised the lake by about 20 metres. Hawea River, which drains the lake, joins the Clutha just downstream of the Albert Town bridge.

Arethusa Pool is couched 150m above Lake Wanaka, near the top of the island of Mou Waho.

Sentinal Peak (1811m) in the McKerrow Range overlooks Lake Hawea. The Neck is out of picture to the left. The brownish areas on the lower slopes are bracken fern, above which are patches of beech forest.

BAXTER AT WANAKA

The Wanaka environment has inspired many poets and artists over the years. James K. Baxter, one of New Zealand's most famous poets, worked on Wanaka Station as a farmhand in 1945. During this time he wrote one of his best-known poems, 'High Country Weather':

Alone we are born
and die alone;
Yet see the red-gold cirrus
over snow-mountain shine.

Upon the upland road
Ride easy, stranger:
Surrender to the sky
Your heart of anger.

ABOVE LEFT: Storm clouds rumble over the western mountains towards Lake Wanaka. OPPOSITE: West Matukituki River. The mountains near the Main Divide are in the distance.

WEATHER WORD

The high mountains away to the west of Wanaka – the Southern Alps – have a big part to play in the climate of the area. Known as the Main Divide, they form a barrier to a relentless procession of moist weather systems approaching from the Tasman Sea. They lift and cool the clouds and wring most of the moisture out of them. This sheltering effect gives rise to Central Otago's subcontinental climate, which is characterised by dry, warm summers and crisp, cold winters.

Wanaka is at the western edge of this climatic zone. Rainfall decreases as you get farther from the mountains. The western side of Lake Wanaka receives about 2000mm of rainfall annually, whereas the town of Wanaka on the other side of the lake – a step farther from the mountains – has an average rainfall of about 700mm. The passage of westerly weather systems across the Main Divide also produces a pattern of warm föhn winds from the northwest. These occur more often in summer and may reach gale force.

Moderated both by the town's proximity to the mountains and the large glacial lake, in Wanaka the summer temperatures typically reach around 25°C and occasionally higher. Frosts occur on about 24 days a year. Despite the adjacent snowclad mountains, in an average year the town can expect snow to lie at lake level on about five days only.

2

TOWN AND AROUND

WHEN THE SUN IS HIGH and the lake a silver mirror, Wanaka is a picturesque, pulsating sort of place. In summertime visitors can outnumber the resident population by at least 10 to one, and in winter skiers and snowboarders make a beeline for the snowline during the day and the bars at night. Even the shoulder seasons can be busy.

Downtown Wanaka resembles a small town that has grown up fast. Some shops are chic and modern; others retain the flavour of Wanaka's small country-town origins. There are more than 30 cafés, restaurants and bars to choose from, many with outdoor seating areas and offering cosmopolitan menus as well as southern New Zealand 'delicacies' such as cheese rolls. The surprisingly wide range of dealer art galleries reflects the town's creative spirit. But although the town's commercial centre has expanded to cater for increasing visitor numbers and a swelling residential population, it remains refreshingly low-rise.

For orientation, a good place to head for is the **Chalmers Street war memorial lookout**. It can be reached via a short sharp climb off Brownston Street, less than 10 minutes' walk from

OPPOSITE: Wanaka's indoor climbing centre is popular on rainy days.
RIGHT: The waterfront area on a fine summer's day.

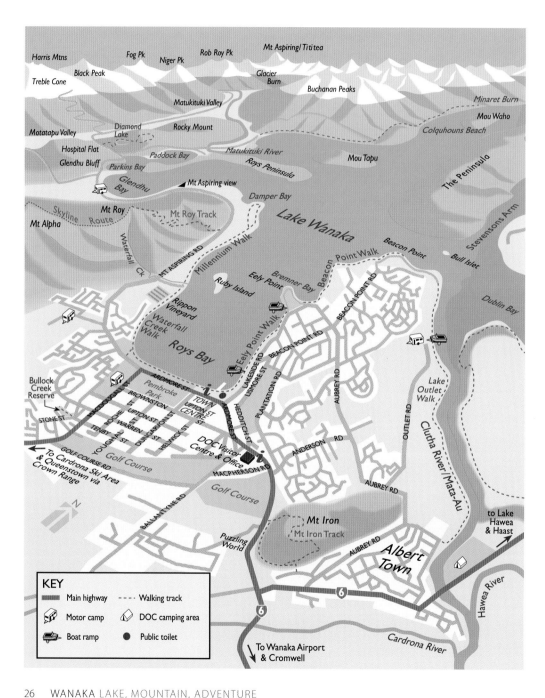

Harris Mtns
Fog Pk
Niger Pk
Rob Roy Pk
Mt Aspiring/Tititea
Black Peak
Treble Cone
Glacier Burn
Buchanan Peaks
Minaret Burn
Mou Waho
Matukituki Valley
Motatapu Valley
Diamond Lake
Rocky Mount
Colquhouns Beach
Hospital Flat
Paddock Bay
Matukituki River
Mou Tapu
Glendhu Bluff
Parkins Bay
Roys Peninsula
The Peninsula
Glendhu Bay
Mt Aspiring view
Damper Bay
Lake Wanaka
Stevensons Arm
Skyline Route
Mt Roy
Mt Roy Track
Beacon Point
Bull Islet
Mt Alpha
Waterfall Ck
MT ASPIRING RD
Millennium Walk
Bremner Bay
Beacon Point Walk
Dublin Bay
Eely Point
BEACON POINT RD
Ruby Island
Eely Point Walk
Rippon Vineyard
Waterfall Creek Walk
Roys Bay
LAKESIDE RD
LISMORE ST
BEACON POINT RD
Bullock Creek Reserve
Pembroke Park
ARDMORE ST
TOWN CENTRE
UPTON ST
AUBREY RD
Lake Outlet Walk
STONE ST
BROWNSTON
MCDOUGALL ST
PLANTATION RD
OUTLET RD
Clutha River/Mata-Au
ST
BROWNSTON ST
UPTON ST
HEDDITCH ST
ROCHE ST
WARREN ST
DUNGARVON ST
ARDMORE ST
TENBY ST
DUNCAN ST
HELWICK ST
To Cardrona Ski Area & Queenstown via Crown Range
GOLF COURSE RD
Golf Course
DOC Visitor Centre & Office
MACPHERSON RD
ANDERSON RD
to Lake Hawea & Haast
BALLANTYNE RD
Golf Course
Mt Iron
Mt Iron Track
AUBREY RD
Puzzling World
AUBREY RD
Albert Town
Hawea River
6
To Wanaka Airport & Cromwell
6
Cardrona River

KEY

Main highway	- - -	Walking track	
Motor camp		DOC camping area	
Boat ramp	●	Public toilet	

the main shopping area. A panorama of the vista can be found there, embedded in the rock, with landmarks named and ready to be checked off when the skyline is clear.

EVENTS CALENDAR

Wanaka's busy events calendar starts with revelry on **New Year's Eve** and a party that often fills the streets down by the lakefront, where alcohol is banned. Live music and fireworks rock in the New Year. Nearby Hawea hosts an eight-hour music festival, also on New Year's Eve. The **Wanaka rodeo** is held in early January, and a **children's holiday programme** runs for two weeks through December and January, offering a diverse range of entertainment and adventures in and around Wanaka and Hawea.

On Thursdays from 3 to 6pm the year-round the **Wanaka artisan market** spreads its colourful tents and interesting goods along the banks of Bullock Creek in the green space just below Lake Wanaka Centre. Arts and crafts, baking and fresh produce from farmers and orchardists are on offer, including cherries, nectarines, apricots and peaches in summer.

In February a crowd-pulling one-day music festival, **Tuki Festival** (formerly Rippon Festival), is held on farmland at Glendhu Bay Station. Music is generated from two stages throughout the day. The event attracts several thousand fans, and proceeds are used to support music education and sustainability projects.

Over three days in February Wanaka hosts New Zealand's largest triathlon event, **Challenge Wanaka**. More than 2000 competitors may be involved in a 3.8km swim, 180km bike ride and 42.2km run, or they may choose to do half the distances. There are sections for children of all ages too. Challenge Wanaka has a multinational air: competitors, including world champion triathletes, typically come from more than 20 countries.

In late summer the **Upper Clutha Agricultural and Pastoral Show** brings the farming world to town. Inaugurated at Cromwell in 1895, it has been held at Wanaka since 1930 and is one of the most popular A&P shows in Otago. It is packed with farm animals, machinery and novelty events, such as the Jack Russell dog race.

The Wanaka artisan market in the downtown area.

Every second year at Easter time Wanaka hosts its biggest event – an international air show called **Warbirds Over Wanaka**, featuring war planes from decades past, right back to World War I. Held at Wanaka Airport, 10km from town, Warbirds attracts enormous numbers of New Zealand and overseas visitors – usually around 50,000 across the three days. For the 30th anniversary airshow in 2018, more than 54,000 attended. It is not uncommon for more than 50 aircraft to appear on the programme.

Since 1989 Wanaka has staged a fascinating annual **Autumn Art School**. Based at Mt Aspiring College during the school holidays, when the autumn days are often crisply stimulating, the art school offers courses as varied as fly-fishing, quiltmaking, bookbinding, nature journalism, furniture construction and oral history recording. Tutors are drawn from around New Zealand and overseas.

In autumn the Roys Bay poplars turn golden and other deciduous trees contribute to warm, vibrant hues around town. It's the portent for a feature attraction, the biennial **Festival of Colour**, when Wanaka showcases a range of artistic events involving talent from New Zealand and abroad. In alternate years there is a weekend-long intellectually stimulating programme of local and international speakers called **Aspiring Conversations**, with the catchline 'It's time for thinking'.

The annual **New Zealand Mountain Film and Book Festival**, established in winter 2002, is a week-long celebration of adventurous outdoor activities in film, art and print. There are screenings in Wanaka, Cromwell and Queenstown.

Wanaka's 2018 Winter Olympians, Zoi Sadowski-Synnott and Nico Porteous, display their gold medals on the Cardrona slopes on their return from the northern hemisphere to a southern summer. GREGOR RICHARDSON/OTAGO DAILY TIMES

Winter is celebrated through a **Winter Games** programme of skiing, snowboarding and snow tricks at skifields in Wanaka and Queenstown. Elite athletes from New Zealand and overseas add status to these games, which also provide local talent with valuable competition. Two Wanaka 16-year-olds went on from this to become Olympic heroes in the 2018 Winter Olympics in South Korea – Zoi Sadowski-Synnott in the women's Big Air snowboard event and Nico Porteous in the men's Freestyle Ski Halfpipe. Both won a bronze medal, becoming the first New Zealanders to win a Winter Olympics medal since 1992.

Spring brings something different – a music festival with character and attitude. Cardrona is the venue, Labour Weekend in October is the time, and the

TOP: Vampire aircraft in low-level flight at the 2014 Wanaka International Airshow. MARTIN DE RUYTER
ABOVE: The Wanaka Airport entrance displays an Italian Aermacchi military jet trainer plane.

WARBIRDS OVER WANAKA

Claiming Southern Hemisphere biggest-and-best status, Warbirds Over Wanaka has a sensational reputation. Begun in 1988 by aviation entrepreneur and businessman Sir Tim Wallis, the first biennial air show and country fair attracted 14,000 visitors. These days the show pulls six or seven times the patronage of that first year. Besides the swooping, soaring aircraft, old and new, with their mixed bag of tricks, the event includes displays of vintage warbirds and machinery and sport aircraft. The stars of the show are invariably the veteran planes.

musical fare is a mix of folk, homegrown and world music. Poets, balladeers and dancers also get a look in, and there is usually an overseas guest artist or two. The faithful followers of the **Cardona Folk Festival** camp in tents, vans and housetrucks in a field beside the historic Cardrona Hall to sing, play and dance. Founded in 1976, this festival is the oldest of its kind in New Zealand still presented annually at the same site.

YEAR-ROUND ATTRACTIONS

Wanaka boasts two cinemas – **Cinema Paradiso** in Brownston Street and **Rubys Cinema and Bar** on Cardrona Valley Road. Established in 1991, Cinema Paradiso is a quirky moviegoers' mecca. It has three theatres with good legroom and a convivial café whose wooden walls are plastered with posters of classic movies. Rubys also serves refreshments, and has a climbing wall available before or after screenings for agile patrons.

Free entertainment for families can be found at the lakefront playground near the information centre and jetty, where there is a dinosaur slide, a shallow swimming pool and a revolving seat. Here you can also watch trout large and small swimming in their Bullock Creek sanctuary adjacent to the playground. Trout and eels also lurk in the shallows around the jetty, waiting for someone to feed them and oblivious to the underwater antics of dainty black New Zealand scaup, the country's only diving duck. Fish and duck food is available from the boat hire business on the beach.

Across the street from the playground – watch carefully for traffic – is the Lake Wanaka Centre, a community facility, and an attractive short walkway gives access to the swift-flowing, spring-fed Bullock Creek. A few minutes' walk up Dunmore Street is Wanaka Library, at 2 Bullock Creek Lane, which presents numerous community activities, especially for children.

Visitors who enjoy golf can use the nearby 18-hole golf course that meanders over the old terminal moraine overlooking the lake, and not far away in Sir Tim Wallis Drive, off Ballantyne Road, is a recreation centre catering for indoor and outdoor sports. Swimmers can choose from the lake or the heated Wanaka Pool next to Mt Aspiring College on Plantation Drive.

Feeding the ducks and gulls at the lakefront.

Puzzling World on the Wanaka–Luggate road opposite Mt Iron has an array of illusions and bewilderment and a complex Great Maze.

The National Transport and Toy Museum is adjacent to Wanaka Airport. Here you can find a massive display of over 30,000 toys and 600 vehicles, including a 32-tonne Centurion tank, cool cars and old fire engines.

Warbirds & Wheels contains a world-class collection of rare and vintage vehicles and a retro café, and is located at Wanaka Airport.

Wanaka Beerworks is next to the transport museum at the airport and offers the opportunity to taste handcrafted beers and tour the aromatic premises.

Basecamp Climbing Centre at 50 Cardrona Valley Road offers rock climbers, new or experienced, a chance to work out on an indoor wall.

CLOCKWISE FROM TOP LEFT: Spring-fed Bullock Creek rushes through Wanaka's downtown area; Puzzling World; the jetty on Wanaka's waterfront.

CAMPING

Wanaka's accommodation options have expanded enormously in recent years. In and around town there are backpackers, a Youth Hostel, bed-and-breakfast lodges, motels, hotels and homestay choices. Camping is also well catered for, and options in the area range from riverside locations with a shared toilet as the only facility, to large motor camps with fully serviced tourist cabins and plenty of amenities.

Wanaka Lakeview Holiday Park is closest to downtown Wanaka, a short walk from the lakefront at the far end of Brownston Street. On Lake Wanaka's western side is Glendhu Bay Motor Camp, 12km from town. The camp offers 1.5km of lakefront and 500 tent sites as well as cabins. It has a reputation as the place to be at Christmas and New Year, and some families have been going to Glendhu Bay for so long their holidaymaking spans a generation or two!

On the way to Glendhu Bay, near the edge of the residential area, there are two holiday parks. Wanaka Kiwi Holiday Park and Motels is at the lake end of Studholme Road, and the Wanaka TOP 10 Holiday Park is a little further along Mt Aspiring Road.

On the other side of town is the Lake Outlet Holiday Park off Aubrey Road, a skipping stone's throw from the river and an auspicious riverbank trout-fishing location. Across the

OPPOSITE: Glendhu Bay from the Roys Peak track. At centre top is Rocky Mountain and to the right the Matukituki River. STUART THORNE

RIGHT, TOP TO BOTTOM: A carpark warning sign at the Wanaka waterfront; Wilkin Valley; Kidds Bush campground.

bridge at Albert Town on the north bank of the Clutha River is a spacious woodland reserve. It spans both sides of the highway adjacent to the Clutha River, with the Hawea River close by. Toilets, picnic tables and a water supply are available here for campers.

Lake Hawea Holiday Park, nestled between State Highway 6 and the lakefront, provides campsites and cabins, and further north on the Haast Pass highway the Makarora Tourist Centre has a range of cabins and tentsites in a tree-clad mountain valley setting.

For campers who require fewer facilities, there are two Department of Conservation camping areas beside State Highway 6 between Lake Hawea and Makarora. A small charge is collected through a self-registration booth. A popular example, Kidds Bush Reserve Campsite, is 30 minutes' drive from Lake Hawea township on a central arm of Lake Hawea. At Kidds Bush, rowan trees join the native mountain beech to provide shade. The area is attractively developed, with a picnic shelter, barbecue facilities, picnic tables, two flush toilets, a water supply and a popular boat ramp. Further north, at Boundary Creek near the head of Lake Wanaka, there is a campsite equipped with toilets and a barbecue area.

So, you have settled in, strolled through the shopping centre and sampled the local food and beverages. You want to widen your horizons – but not by walking or boating or taking to the air. Where can you drive to?

DRIVES

Roads radiate in just about every direction from Wanaka, inviting easy half-day trips on tarseal with nothing more strenuous than lunch, afternoon tea or a picnic on the programme. Here are a few options:

CLOCKWISE FROM TOP LEFT: Some of the names on the pioneer memorial at the Albert Town reserve on the north side of the Clutha River; Cardrona Hall; Cardrona Distillery and Museum director Desiree Whitaker; the Cardrona Hotel, a popular stopping place for day-trippers.

Motatapu Valley. From Glendhu Bay there is a road as far as the gorge in the distance.

Albert Town: A short hop from Wanaka, Albert Town offers numerous picnic places on the banks of New Zealand's biggest river. Down Wicklow Terrace is a grassed area offering a local history lesson through information panels. On the north side of the Albert Town bridge a reserve and campground straddle the highway and provide access to the Hawea and Clutha rivers. There is a memorial cairn to nineteenth-century settlers here.

Cardrona: Twenty minutes' drive south up the Cardrona Valley is the historic 1863 Cardrona Hotel, dating from the goldrush days and offering refreshments, accommodation and a pleasant beer garden. Across the road from the Cardrona Alpine Resort access road is Cardrona Distillery, which has a café and a small museum. Founded in 2015, the distillery laid its first whisky cask in November that year. The distillery's first release of 10-year-old single malt is anticipated in 2025. The business offers tours of the gleaming steel and copper vats and distilling apparatus, and indoor avenues of American oak barrels.

Tuohys Lagoon and the road to Glendhu Bay in the early 20th century.

A.H. MCLAREN PHOTO ALBUM, UCHRS

KEEPING IN TOUCH

Wanaka's free weekly newspaper, *The Wanaka Sun*, is locally owned and operated and publishes regional news and informative articles. Copies are distributed around the region, or you can find it online at www.thewanakasun.co.nz.

The *Upper Clutha Messenger* is a community bulletin that appears on Wednesdays, free and brimming with details of what is happening in town and the surrounding district: www.mymessenger.co.nz

Radio Wanaka 92.2 FM runs local news, weather and community notices.

Glendhu Bay: About 10 minutes' drive from downtown Wanaka, due west on Mount Aspiring Road, Glendhu Bay has a scenic lake and mountain setting and high-country farming atmosphere. Although it has no cafés, it offers a feast for the eyes, with views of Tititea/Mt Aspiring ('Glistening Peak') a notable reward on a clear day. Take care while driving, as the pull-off area is on the lake side of the highway and rushes into view without much warning.

Lake Hawea: About 15 minutes along State Highway 6 from Wanaka is the village of Lake Hawea. Like its more illustrious neighbour, the township is built on a terminal moraine overlooking a large glacial lake and attracts a swag of summer holidaymakers. But there the similarity ends, for Lake Hawea is a relatively small, one-of-everything village, and local folk like it that way. Food outlets include a hotel and café. A recreational feature of the village is its lakefront reserve, the esplanade, where picnic tables and a gravel beach invite a stopover on days when the northwest föhn wind is not cutting up rough. A stroll over the dam at the lake outlet is instructive.

Luggate: Ten minutes from Wanaka by car on the main road to Cromwell, Luggate is a lively settlement with more shops and facilities than its stock of houses would suggest.

Makarora: For more than half the 45-minute drive to Makarora, the highway north towards Haast Pass and the West Coast follows a lakeshore – first Lake Hawea, then, over the Neck, Lake Wanaka. Of all the drives out of Wanaka it provides the most dramatic scenery. Makarora has two tearooms several kilometres apart. The main settlement has a motor camp and a small Department of Conservation visitor centre that provides information on local walks, the nearby national park and the saga of the Haast Pass highway.

Tarras: East of Wanaka (turn left off State Highway 6 just past Wanaka Airport) is the little farming settlement of Tarras, where a café and craft shop signal its location on a tourist route: State Highway 8 over the Lindis Pass to the Mackenzie Country and the Aoraki/Mt Cook region.

The Clutha River above the Red Bridge, Luggate.

After your drive, you are back in the mountain cradle called Wanaka. If it is summer there will still be a lot of daylight left. You might choose to enjoy a late-afternoon drink outdoors at a café or bar downtown as the sparrows fidget at your feet, checking for crumbs. Wanaka is a paradise for them, too.

PEMBROKE PARK

A symbol of green spaciousness, Pembroke Park – on the other side of Ardmore Street from Roys Bay Recreation Reserve – is a breath of fresh air for a town under pressure to expand in all directions. Its undeveloped state speaks of a community not ready to concede everything to development. Since the early 1970s there have been repeated proposals for a community centre to be built on the site, but nothing has eventuated except for carparking developments at the shopping centre end of the park.

A bronze plaque erected in the year 2000 declares the 10ha park to be 'for the enjoyment of residents and visitors'. At the time, a range of community groups and organisations, including local authorities, put their names to the declaration and undertook tree plantings.

Pembroke Park has long been controversial.

The land was made a reserve in 1948 – the year government agencies revealed a plan to build a hydroelectric dam in the Luggate area that would raise Lake Wanaka by 2.4m. Three-quarters of the park area was set aside for use by the New Zealand Electricity Department. However, when the scheme was revisited in the 1960s local people opposed it. They mounted a campaign under the slogan 'Hands Off Lake Wanaka' (HOWL), and in 1972 they convinced the government to abandon the dam idea. Today an Act of parliament enshrines the natural condition of Lake Wanaka, and a statutory body, the Guardians of Lake Wanaka, makes sure it stays that way.

Control of the Pembroke Park reserve eventually passed to the local council. The only way it can be flooded now is through naturally high lake levels.

3

A REGION MADE FOR WALKING AND CYCLING

WANAKA is a walkers' and cyclists' paradise, offering a range of opportunities from short, easy tracks to challenging trails that will test fitness and endurance.

The Upper Clutha Tracks Trust has been steadily developing new tracks in conjunction with the Department of Conservation and the district council. Ultimately, a connected trail the length of the Clutha River – from its source at Wanaka to Clutha Mouth and the Pacific Ocean in South Otago – is envisaged by the Clutha Mata-Au River Parkway group.

Te Araroa Trail, a walking route that stretches the length of the country from Cape Reinga to Bluff, passes through this region using the tracks that hug the Hawea and Upper Clutha rivers, the southern shores of Lake Wanaka and the Motatapu track.

It is wise to carry drinking water, especially on the longer walks or in hot weather, and some energy food is important as well on the harder tracks. At high altitudes the weather can change rapidly, so always pack warm gear for expeditions into the mountains.

The risk of fire is real, particularly on the tracks east of Wanaka where the climate and environs are drier, and prohibited fire seasons are commonly declared in summer. A single spark can cause havoc by destroying grassland, shrubland and regenerating bush.

A few of the walking tracks in the Wanaka region are circuits; most require you to backtrack at least some of the way. Distances and times given here are one-way only. The times are for walkers; they are approximate and do not allow for very many stops. Each track is ranked as easy, moderate or hard. Dogs are allowed on all tracks unless specified otherwise.

OPPOSITE: Biking the Upper Clutha River Track near Albert Town.
RIGHT: A sylvan setting by the Clutha River near Luggate.

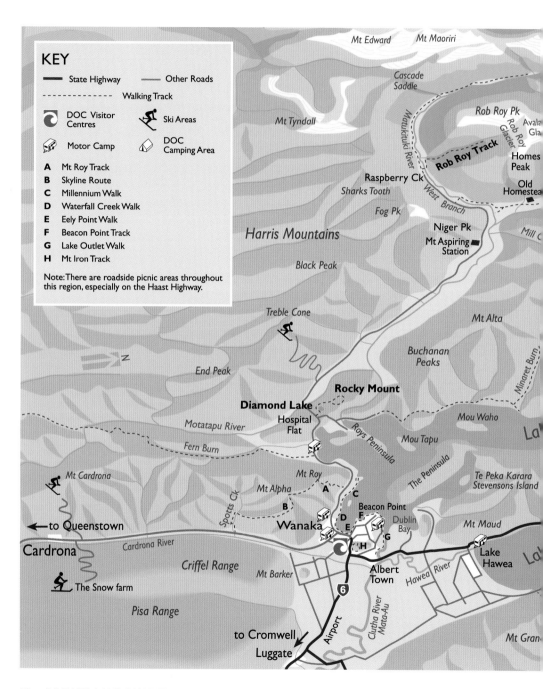

KEY

━━━━ State Highway   ──── Other Roads

- - - - - - - - - - Walking Track

◐ DOC Visitor Centres   🎿 Ski Areas

🚐 Motor Camp   ⛺ DOC Camping Area

A Mt Roy Track
B Skyline Route
C Millennium Walk
D Waterfall Creek Walk
E Eely Point Walk
F Beacon Point Track
G Lake Outlet Walk
H Mt Iron Track

Note: There are roadside picnic areas throughout this region, especially on the Haast Highway.

Mt Edward   Mt Maoriri

Cascade Saddle

Rob Roy Pk

Avala Gla

Mt Tyndall

Rob Roy Track

Homes Peak

Raspberry Ck

Old Homestea

Sharks Tooth

Fog Pk

West Branch

Matukituki River

Rob Roy Glacier

Niger Pk

Mill C

Harris Mountains

Mt Aspiring Station

Black Peak

Treble Cone

Mt Alta

Buchanan Peaks

End Peak

Rocky Mount

Minaret Burn

Diamond Lake

Mou Waho

Motatapu River

Hospital Flat

Roys Peninsula

Mou Tapu

La

Fern Burn

The Peninsula

Te Peka Karara Stevensons Island

Mt Cardrona

Mt Roy

Mt Alpha

Spotts Ck

A

C

to Queenstown

B

Beacon Point

D

F

Dublin Bay

Mt Maud

Cardrona

Wanaka

E

G

Cardrona River

H

Lake Hawea

La

Criffel Range

Mt Barker

Albert Town

Hawea River

The Snow farm

6

to Cromwell

Luggate

Pisa Range

Airport

Clutha River Mata-Au

Mt Gran

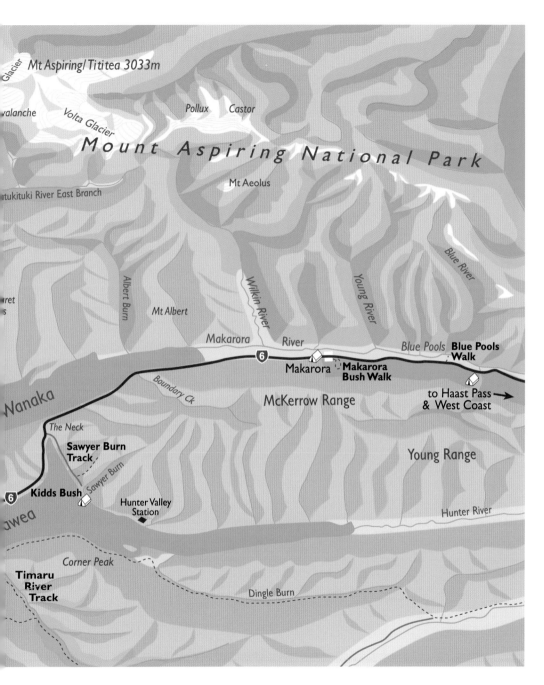

Glacier

Mt Aspiring/ Tititea 3033m

valanche   Volta Glacier   Pollux   Castor

M o u n t A s p i r i n g N a t i o n a l P a r k

Mt Aeolus

atukituki River East Branch

Blue River

ret   Mt Albert   *Albert Burn*   *Wilkin River*   *Young River*

Makarora   River   *Blue Pools* **Blue Pools Walk**

Makarora   **Makarora Bush Walk**

Wanaka   *Boundary Ck*   McKerrow Range   to Haast Pass →
& West Coast

The Neck

Sawyer Burn Track   Young Range

Sawyer Burn

Kidds Bush   Hunter Valley Station   Hunter River

awea

Corner Peak

Timaru River Track   Dingle Burn

TOWN WALKS

Eely Point *1.5km, 15 mins, easy*

This walkway links the marina area near the town centre with Eely Point on the eastern side of Roys Bay. Sheltered from the prevailing northwest winds, the walk is picked up beyond the marina buildings and follows the wooded shoreline to Eely Point reserve, where large conifers create an open woodland area on the small peninsula. In summer the beaches here are popular for swimming, boating and picnicking. Cycling is allowed on this track, and riders should give way to pedestrians.

The track continues as a vehicle road beyond Eely Point for about 500m to Bremner Bay, another popular bathing/boating beach.

Beacon Point and lake outlet *4km, 1 hr, easy*

From Bremner Bay (Aubrey Road) on the north side of Eely Point reserve, a level walkway/cycleway leads to Penrith Beach, Beacon Point and the lake outlet. Contrasting environments flank the track on the way to Penrith Beach. On the left you will see glimpses of the lake shoreline through mānuka, kōwhai and other native trees; on the right are large architecturally designed residential and holiday homes with expansive gardens.

Penrith Beach has a wide and welcoming gravel beach backed by Lombardy poplars and is one of Wanaka's favoured swimming areas, although it is exposed to northwest winds. From Penrith Beach you can join Beacon Point Road, which skirts around the shoreline to Beacon Point, 2.5km from Bremner Bay. The beacon referred to is a red light warning boats to keep clear of a cluster of rocks near the shore. The lake outlet – genesis of the Clutha River/ Mata-Au – and Lake Outlet Holiday Park are about 1.5km further on. Outlet Road offers an alternative route back to town.

TOP: Forested Eely Point lies beyond the marina. ABOVE: The Upper Clutha River Track offers a close encounter with New Zealand's largest river.

Lake outlet to Albert Town *3km, 50 mins, easy*

Following the riverbank almost all the way, this walkway/cycleway allows you to experience the birthplace of New Zealand's largest river, the Clutha/Mata-Au. The track is suitable for all ages and is mainly flat with a few gentle undulations. Mountain bikes are recommended for this track, and cyclists should watch for pedestrians where visibility is limited.

The river is deep, clear and swirling from the outset, and flows average 200 cubic metres per second. There are good views of rapids about halfway to Albert Town. Along the way, willows, poplars and pines are mixed with native trees and shrubs, and most of the upstream end of the track is shaded and agreeably cool in summer. Fantails, grey warblers, bellbirds and New Zealand pigeons are common in the area.

The track also provides access for anglers, and painted posts indicate the fishing zone. Only fly-fishing is permitted over the first kilometre of the river.

To get to the outlet end of the track, take Anderson Road, Aubrey Road and Outlet Road (follow the signs to the holiday park). The end of Outlet Road is roughly formed and the carpark and information kiosk are down by the river.

Waterfall Creek *2km, 35 mins, easy*

From the southwest corner of Roys Bay this walkway/cycleway skirts Wanaka Station Park and the stately grounds of the old Wanaka Station homestead, staying fairly close to the lake all the way to Waterfall Creek. The track rises gently in places and passes the generous lawns of Edgewater Resort and the lower end of Rippon Vineyard. Poplars and willows (including the renowned tree) line the track early on and give way to shrubland featuring mānuka bushes as

the track nears Waterfall Creek. Fantails sometimes flutter across your path, seeking a feed of flying insects you might have disturbed. In summer the many little beaches along the shoreline are visited by boaties enjoying picnics and perhaps a day out with waterskis.

The Waterfall Creek delta, opposite Ruby Island, is a popular spot for launching canoes, kayaks and motorboats, with road access available from the Wanaka–Glendhu Bay road. The delta is a fun place for children, who like making shapes in gravel brought down by the creek that tumbles swiftly to the lake. The eponymous waterfall is located above the road to Glendhu Bay.

The photo point near Waterfall Creek looking back to Mt Iron.

Wanaka Millennium Track *3.5km, 1 hr, moderate*

About 100m from the shoreline at Waterfall Creek, a bridge marks the start of Wanaka Millennium Track, a popular trail for both walkers and mountain bikers that leads to Ironside Hill and Damper Bay and continues on from there to Glendhu Bay. The track negotiates bluffs that rise from the lake, and short climbs are rewarded by sweeping views of the lake and mountains and back towards the town of Wanaka. It also offers a good perspective of Ruby Island, which lies 600m off the mouth of Waterfall Creek.

Information panels are located at various points along the way, providing insight into the nature and human history of the area. Ironside Hill is the landmark for this section of the track (see 'Longer walks'). Revegetation of the track edges has been undertaken in recent years by community groups.

Bullock Creek Hatchery Spring *340m, 6 min, easy*

A raised boardwalk around a spring-fed wetland that is the source of Bullock Creek was opened in 2018. Located between Stone Street and a new subdivision, the walkway winds around the wetland of a decommissioned hatchery for brown and rainbow trout. It was built by the Otago Fish and Game Council and Queenstown Lakes District Council with support from the Wanaka Residents' Association and Te Kakano Aotearoa Trust. Weeds were cleared from the 2.5 ha of wetland and hundreds of native trees, shrubs and wetland species were planted.

Mt Iron *2km, 50 mins, moderate*

A sloping hill with impressive all-round views, Mt Iron is the highest landmark close to Wanaka. The route climbs 240m to reach the flat summit (50 minutes) by way of a zigzagging track.

You can walk a circuit on this track, and there are two possible starting points. The well-signposted main entrance is from a carpark beside the highway into town, about 2km from the lakefront. The second access point is located opposite Puzzling World. Parking is available under the trees. From here you follow the track in an anticlockwise direction around the hill. The climb is steeper this way but you are likely to reach the summit 5–10 minutes sooner. Allow a good 2 hours for the round trip, including time at the top to rest and enjoy the panorama.

From the summit there are glorious views – northwest over the town, lake and Southern Alps foothills to Tititea/Mt Aspiring, south to the Cardrona Valley, southeast over the Upper Clutha valley to the Dunstan Mountains, and northeast over Albert Town to Lake Hawea.

Kānuka, of similar appearance to mānuka (tea tree) but taller, is the most common tree on Mt Iron. The leaves of both species exude a juniper-like fragrance when crushed. Bush birds are reasonably common here, and brown creeper, a South Island endemic species, is worth

Joggers on the Millennium Track near Waterfall Creek.

watching out for. These social little birds, which have a distinctive undulating trill, trickle about the canopy in flocks feeding on insects and fruit.

Mt Iron was named by Wanaka Station owner Robert Wilkin after Ironhurst in Dumfries, Scotland, and the reserve here was created in 1905. The hill is a classic example of a rôche moutonnée (sheep rock), a mound shaped by glaciation. Through a process of 'plucking' embedded ice, glaciers through the ages have smoothed the western, upstream side of Mt Iron and left the eastern side craggy and steep.

LONGER TRACKS

Millennium Track: Waterfall Creek to Glendhu Bay *12.5km, 3–4 hrs, moderate*
A popular mountain-bike experience involving several steep sections, this trail is also a highlight for walkers, who get more time to savour the scenery – lake, islands, peninsulas and Alps – as the track curves slowly around the cliffs in the vicinity of Ironside Hill. Soon you are at Damper Bay, a snug gravel beach and swimming spot.

The second half of the track mostly follows the shoreline through shrubland until you reach Glendhu Bay Motor Camp.

Roys Peak *8km, 2.5–3 hrs, hard*

To enjoy this classic climb you need to be fit. With its zigzags stretched out the track measures 8km, and from the foot-of-the-mountain starting point to the summit you will climb more than 1200m. The track is accessed from a signposted carpark beside Mount Aspiring Road, 6km from town. Such is the social-media hubbub about this walk, your first challenge might be to find space in the carpark.

The track follows a four-wheel-drive farm road virtually all the way. At the ridge below the summit you have a choice of following the road or taking a steeper and more direct trail up the ridge. At this height you might be above the clouds and paragliders can often be seen sidling around the slopes below.

The views from the summit are breathtaking – Tititea/Mt Aspiring and the Matukituki Valley, the Harris Mountains, the lake and town, Hawea Flat and Lake Hawea and beyond. At this height, 1581m above sea level, you feel like you are flying.

Always pack windproof warm clothing, as even in mid-summer the summit can be a cold place and is exposed to sudden changes in the weather. Temperatures are likely to drop significantly after dusk, and snow often lies for a couple of months in winter and spring. The buildings here are mainly for telecommunication purposes – there is no shelter for trekkers.

Note that the track is closed in spring (1 October to 10 November) to allow for lambing. It crosses farmland and access is provided through the cooperation of the owner. Leave all gates as you find them; dogs and mountain bikes are not permitted. Winter and spring snowfalls can produce avalanches.

Skyline Track: For really fit trekkers, a lengthy alternative route back to Wanaka involves following the summit ridge south through to Mt Alpha and down Spotts Creek to a poled route leading to the Cardrona Valley. You cross 11km of farmland after leaving Roys Peak, and from the exit point on Cardrona Valley Road it is 10km back to town. The Skyline Track is for advanced trampers only. The route is not recommended in winter. There is no water or shade, and there are risks of snow avalanches in spring. This route is not recommended in winter and at other times can be affected by cloudy conditions.

Diamond Lake/Rocky Mountain
Lake circuit: 2.5km, 45 mins return, easy
Lake lookout: 500m from the lake circuit, 30 mins, moderate
Rocky Mountain summit: 7km, 3 hrs return, hard

A 19km drive along the road to Glendhu Bay from downtown Wanaka brings you to the turn-off and carpark for Diamond Lake, an elevated glacial lake that lies at the foot of Rocky Mountain.

ABOVE: Mt Roy (1581m) seen from the northwest, overlooking Glendhu and Parkins bays. Roys Peak is accessed from the other side. RIGHT: Fuchsia flowers overhang the track to the Diamond Lake lookout. BOTTOM: Diamond Lake is perched above the Motatapu Valley.

A zigzag track from the carpark takes you up to a terrace by the lake, where the circuit track is marked.

From the lake the lookout track rises steeply through native bush featuring the world's largest tree fuchsia, kōtukutuku or *Fuchsia excorticata*, easily recognised by its peeling pale-orange bark. The dainty purple 'ballerina' flowers with their bright-blue pollen arrive after the leaves return in spring, and the little purple drupes (kōnini) are delicious.

From the lookout, on a precipice high above the lake, you can carry on along the track to a low

viewpoint over Lake Wanaka, or follow the signs to the summit of Rocky Mountain, a longer hike on a looptrack.

By the time you reach the summit cairn (777m), you have climbed about 450m from the carpark into a tundra-like subalpine environment. The flat schist rocks provide good seats and the views are especially good from mid-afternoon, when the lowering sun accentuates the braided Matukituki River far below as it nears the lake. The two largest islands of Lake Wanaka, Mou Waho and Mou Tapu, stand out in the view, and on a clear day you can see Tititea/Mt Aspiring and over the Motatapu Valley to the Harris Mountains and Treble Cone skifield. New Zealand pipits, small rangeland ground-feeding birds, often provide company at the summit.

The track carries on down the Lake Wanaka side of Rocky Mountain to return you to the Diamond Lake lookout and the way back to the carpark.

This popular route crosses farmland, and access is provided through the cooperation of the owners. The track is maintained by volunteers, and materials are mainly paid for by donations from users. Mountain bikes and dogs are not allowed.

TOP: From the summit of Rocky Mountain there is a spectcular view of the Matukituki River and Lake Wanaka. SOPHORA PEAT MIDDLE: A fruiting coprosma bush beside the Diamond Lake track. ABOVE: Snowberry flowers on the slopes of Rocky Mountain.

Rob Roy Valley *5km, 1.5–2 hrs, moderate*

This track is popular with those who relish a challenging walk to access an alpine environment without the bother of a large pack.

The track sets out from Raspberry Creek carpark at the end of Mount Aspiring Road, 54km from Wanaka. The last few kilometres of gravel road involve fording several creeks, some of which may become impassable during heavy rain or snowmelt.

From the carpark, the first 15 minutes of walking is across farmland to a swing bridge over the churning West Branch of the Matukituki River. Once across the river you are in Mount Aspiring National Park. The track climbs steadily through beech forest, a refreshing place to be on a warm day, and provides glimpses of Rob Roy Stream tumbling down its deep gorge. A lookout 30 minutes below the treeline offers views of the river, glacier and waterfalls.

Stunted beech trees and a belt of deciduous mountain ribbonwood form the treeline at 730m, where there is a lookout with information panels. By this stage you have walked about 4km from the swing bridge and gained 330m in elevation. The large waterfall to the left has a drop of over 200m. The upper part of the Rob Roy Valley is an alpine meadow

TOP: A swingbridge over the West Matukituki River gives walking access to the subalpine Rob Roy Valley.
RIGHT: Rob Roy Stream plunges through beech forest. Above the rock wall is the Rob Roy Glacier.

TOP: A kea above the treeline in the Rob Roy Valley. ABOVE: The Matukituki River meets Lake Wanaka – a view from the Minaret Burn Track. Roys Peak forms a backdrop.

where the yellow daisy-like flowers of invasive hieracium or hawkweed are conspicuous in summer.

High on a rock shelf on the western side of the valley is the Rob Roy Glacier and, above it, Rob Roy Peak (2606m), the fifth highest mountain in the national park. Here you are rubbing shoulders with the Southern Alps, and on a fine day you can easily spend an hour soaking in the alpine atmosphere. Watch out for the inquisitive mountain parrot/kea and the New Zealand falcon/kārearea. Please do not feed the kea. Human foods can be harmful to them and they are prone to accidents involving man-made objects. Besides, they can quickly become annoying to people and damage their cars.

From Raspberry Creek carpark a longer day trip can be made up the grassy flats of the West Matukituki Valley to Aspiring Hut, a base for climbers and trampers. Owned by the New Zealand Alpine Club, the hut is an attractive stone building about 9km from the road end. Allow 5–6 hours for the return trip; dogs are not allowed.

Minaret Burn, Colquhouns Beach
7km, 2–3 hrs, moderate
Accessed from the end of West Wanaka Road, 5km west of Glendhu Bay, this track sets out from Homestead Bay on West Wanaka Station and skirts the lake shoreline and headlands for much of the way. The track is narrow in places at first and passes through shrubland and bracken fern until it meets a four-wheel-drive track. After about a three-hour walk from Homestead Bay a side track leads down to Colquhouns Beach, a nice place for a picnic and swim on a fine summer's day.

From Colquhouns, longer and more demanding tracks continue on to Station Creek Conservation Area and, via Rumbling Burn, to the Mt Alpha Conservation Area. Minaret Burn is further on.

Kidds Bush *1km, 30 mins, moderate*

Nestled at the foot of the McKerrow Range on the western side of Lake Hawea, Kidds Bush is a popular campsite and recreational spot. To get there, head north on State Highway 6 – the road to Hawea, Makarora and the West Coast – and turn right into unsealed Mead Road after 37km, just before the highway climbs to go over the Neck. A 6km drive leads to Kidds Bush Recreation Reserve, where there is a designated Department of Conservation campsite with toilets, a day shelter and barbecue facilities.

From the camp, a nature-walk looptrack climbs through the beech forest to about 50m above the lake before angling back to the camp. Mountain beech dominates the canopy, and wineberry, lemonwood, marbleleaf, kōhūhū and tree fuchsia are prominent understorey trees. In December the forest is usually ablaze with perched clumps of the native *Peraxilla* mistletoe. The crimson-flowered clumps of mistletoe are attached to the beech trees and make a startling contrast amid so much greenery. Many of the trees and shrubs on the nature walk were planted in 1993 by the Department of Conservation and community groups.

Sheltered from westerly winds, Kidds Bush has long been a favourite spot for outdoor enthusiasts. It was declared a reserve in 1891. Rainfall here is relatively low – 900mm a year compared to Makarora's 2500mm. Note that sandflies can be a nuisance, especially on warm, calm, overcast days.

TOP: Mountain beech regeneration at Kidds Bush reserve. ABOVE: The veined leaf patterns of a common forest tree, marbleleaf, known to Māori as putaputawētā.

Sawyer Burn *3km, 1.5 hrs, hard*

A tougher challenge than the Kidds Bush nature walk, the Sawyer Burn track sets out from the same spot. It follows a ridge most of the way, straight up through the beech forest to the treeline. The Sawyer Burn occupies the valley to the right, its name recalling the milling of indigenous forest in this area over 100 years ago. From the treeline the views of Lake Hawea and the mountains cradling it are outstanding. Lake Hawea's main tributary is the 41km-long Hunter River, which enters the lake at its northern end.

Above the treeline there is an old musterer's hut with two bunks and an open fireplace. It provides something of a destination if you are keen to walk further, not to mention a place where you may want to catch your breath. At least the lakeshore sandflies are not troublesome there.

MAKARORA SHORT WALKS

Makarora Bush *400m, 15 mins, easy*

At Makarora, 64km from Wanaka on the Haast Pass Highway, a short walk through a remnant stand of podocarp and silver beech forest is a great way to stretch your legs after a spell of driving. The entrance is a short distance north of the Department of Conservation's Makarora base. Flat all the way, the track wanders through a forest of mataī, kahikatea and rimu trees, some of which are impressively large.

Along the way you pass a pitsaw facility that illustrates how timber was sawn in the early days. The track emerges at the Makarora campground, from where you can loop back to the carpark.

Blue Pools *750m, 30 mins, easy*

The Blue Pools track meanders gently down through magnificent beech forest before crossing a swing bridge over the Makarora River. There, a viewing platform overlooks the ice-blue pools of crystal-clear water near the mouth of Blue River, where it emerges from a tight gorge. Rainbow and brown trout are sometimes seen patrolling the pools, and in the riverbed below the boardwalk visitors have built cairns and other artistic structures from the river-worn rocks.

Access is off State Highway 6, 8km north of Makarora village and 72km from Wanaka. Carparking can be an issue, and pedestrians should beware of traffic as they cross the highway.

FURTHER INFORMATION

More detailed information and maps of these and other walks are available from the Department of Conservation visitor centres at Wanaka, Makarora and Haast.

Native birds here include the rifleman, fantail, grey warbler, brown creeper, and the threatened mohua or yellowhead, a canary-yellow songster.

CYCLING

The Wanaka region has plenty of options for biking, whether you are a road cyclist, an off-road mountain biker or a trick rider.

In town there are at least two bikeparks. Lismore Park, on the high ground immediately north of downtown Wanaka, has a set of jumps and undulating terrain; and near the Forest Heights subdivision is Sticky Forest, a pine plantation with a circuit for intermediate and advanced riders.

There are over 750km of mountain-bike tracks in the wider Wanaka region. You can ride all the way from Glendhu Bay to Luggate via tracks that hug the lakeshore and riverbank, and the Upper Clutha River track from Albert Town to Luggate's Red Bridge is a scenic treat. From the Red Bridge end you can enjoy an easy ride along terraces above the river before dropping down for a close encounter with the amazing blue-green Clutha – a thrilling experience.

From Albert Town, take the bridge across the river to the north bank, turn left and try out a circuit that takes in Dublin Bay and the Clutha River from near the lake outlet. The purpose-built Deans Bank track, offering humps, hollows and berms, follows

Blue pools, Makarora Valley.

A CODE OF CONDUCT FOR OFF-ROAD CYCLISTS

- Wear a helmet.
- Give way to walkers, regardless of circumstances.
- Assume there is someone around each bend and slow down accordingly.
- Pass with care, and let others know well in advance if you are approaching from behind.

the river's north bank. Cycle tracks also lead to Lake Hawea from the camping ground on the north bank at Albert Town (turn right after crossing the bridge to join the Hawea River Track).

During summer the chairlifts at Cardrona and Treble Cone skifields provide access to what are reputedly New Zealand's highest bikeparks, above 2000m, which cover areas that are ski trails in winter. Farther afield, mountain-bike excursions into the west and east branches of the Matukituki Valley are recommended for experienced riders. The West Matukituki ride covers 18km return from the road end at Raspberry Creek to Aspiring Hut.

For those who like to be competitive, the annual 47km Motatapu race is a challenging event. Starting at Glendhu Bay and ending at Arrowtown, the route traverses several high-country stations and has steep climbs and descents and a fair number of river crossings. The route was used by early Māori on seasonal journeys inland, and by European gold prospectors in the 1860s.

Bikers who want an extra level of excitement can opt for a guided heli-mountain-biking ride on various mountains.

ABOVE: Rock climbing at Hospital Flat close to Mt Aspiring Road.
OPPOSITE: Tititea/Mt Aspiring towers over the West Matukituki Valley. A speargrass (*Aciphylla*) is flowering in the foreground.

CLIMBING

Mount Aspiring National Park offers challenges aplenty for climbers. The mountains east of the national park and facing Wanaka, including Black Peak, Mt Alta, Buchanan Peaks and Minaret Peaks, are over 2000m in height and snow-clad through much of winter and spring. Black Peak (2289m) in the Harris Mountains stands out in the late afternoon light. It is sometimes mistaken for Tititea/ Mt Aspiring (3033m), the ultimate challenge for climbers in this region.

Rock climbers can enjoy a great day at indoor facilities in the town. Outdoors, guided climbing tours are available, or you can venture out to Hospital Flat, just five minutes' drive past Glendhu Bay on Mount Aspiring Road, where cliffs along the edge of the paddocks provide attractive climbing walls. Incidentally, the valley's name has nothing to do with rock climbing injuries; it was a place where tired or injured horses were kept in the days before motor transport.

4

WATER, AIR AND SNOW

ON THE WATER

Wanaka is brimming with water-based activities. You can jetboat, raft, sledge (riverboard), canyon, kayak and canoe local rivers. Regular jetboat trips use the Upper Clutha River, and jetboats can also be chartered. Rafts travel for up to 45km on the Upper Clutha following the route taken by log rafts during the nineteenth-century goldfields days. Canyoning, which is not for the faint-hearted, involves hurtling along in fast-flowing water, plunging down water-polished chutes and abseiling waterfalls.

Lake cruises echoing the very roots of Wanaka tourism offer trips out to Mou Waho, the outermost island, where you are guided on foot to the pool at the summit – just as in the old days.

In the Makarora area you can have a three-in-one adventure called the Siberia Experience, which involves flying into the Siberia Valley, walking out to the Wilkin River and jetboating back to base.

For those who have their own boats, there are five-knot speed zones in the upper reaches of the Clutha River and throughout the Hawea River. Restrictions also apply in Roys Bay – the area immediately in front of the town. A useful publication is the *Lakes Wanaka & Hawea Boating Guide*, published by the Queenstown Lakes District Council and available at information centres and on the council website. It is packed with maps and information about boat ramps, low-speed zones, waterskiing restrictions and ski lanes, navigation lights and safe boating practices.

OPPOSITE: Canoeing on the Motatapu River.
RIGHT: A busy summer's day on the western side of Roys Bay.

WANAKA'S ISLANDS

Lake Wanaka has four significant islands – Mou Waho, Mou Tapu, Te Peka Karara (Stevensons) and Ruby Island – and all are public reserves, uninhabited and open to visitors. Dogs are not allowed on any of the islands, and a year-round fire ban applies.

The largest are Mou Waho (140ha) and Mou Tapu (117ha), which are located on the long axis of the lake. Mou Waho, meaning 'outer island', is 16km from town, and Mou Tapu ('sacred island') is 11km from the marina and partly visible from it.

Popular with visitors since the nineteenth century, **Mou Waho** was formerly known as Harwich Island and, in earlier times, Pigeon or Manuka Island. It has a lovely tree-clad beach and picnic area with a toilet and barbecue facilities, and the walk from there to Arethusa Pool is delightful. The little lake, also known

'DUCK ITCH'

A seasonal skin ailment known as 'duck itch' occasionally affects people swimming and paddling in Lake Wanaka, causing a skin irritation, the medical name of which is *Schistosome dermatitis*. The pathogen, a tiny parasite transmitted by native water snails and ducks, can cause itchy spots followed sometimes by lumps that may persist for several days.

OPPOSITE: A view north over Lake Wanaka and the islands of Mou Tapu and Mou Waho. STUART THORNE RIGHT: Enjoying a fine day above Arethusa Pool on Mou Waho. In the distance, beyond the Neck, is a glimpse of Lake Hawea. ECO WANAKA ADVENTURES MIDDLE: A buff weka, typically curious, approaches a visitor on the island of Mou Waho. ECO WANAKA ADVENTURES BOTTOM: Shags on a Roys Bay rock try drying their wings in weak winter sun.

as Moutimu, nestles at the top of the island about 150m above the main lake. Introduced conifer trees dominate the southern and eastern sides of the island. Just north of Mou Waho is the deepest part of Lake Wanaka, a basin reaching 311m – some 33m below sea level.

Mou Tapu, formerly called Crescent Island, is steeper and harder to access by boat. There are few safe landing places and no beaches comparable to Mou Waho's. Crescent-shaped, it rises to 200m. Its native forest is impressively intact compared to the other islands, with rātā, kōwhai, broadleaf, cabbage tree and mānuka prominent. There are no formed tracks or facilities on Mou Waho.

Te Peka Karara/Stevensons Island (65ha) is 11km from town and about halfway up Stevensons Arm. More sheltered from wind and waves than the larger islands, it is popular with picnickers and campers. The main landing place is a 200m-wide gravel

Ruby Island and Mt Iron from the Millennium Track near Waterfall Creek.

beach that is sheltered from the prevailing northwest wind. It has a roomy flat area behind it, a toilet and barbecue facilities. Sparsely vegetated **Bull Islet**, small and low enough to be covered with spray in stormy conditions, lies near the entrance of Stevensons Island.

Ruby Island (3ha), less than 2km from town, is a superb destination for canoeists, kayakers and boaties. Waterfall Creek is the nearest mainland launching place. The Ruby Island Management Committee, a keen volunteer group, has installed a jetty, gas barbecue and toilet on behalf of the Queenstown Lakes District Council, which manages the island. A track around it provides great views of the lake, mountains and town, and allows visitors to see how well the island's guardians have managed a revegetation project following a disastrous fire in 1992.

The walk passes a unique piece of history – the foundations of a wooden dance floor near the top of the island, which was originally sprung with the aid of hundreds of old car tyres. In the late 1920s Ruby Island hosted a cabaret on Saturday nights, and on New Year's Eve up to 300 revellers were ferried over from town to eat and dance to gramophone music. The return boat trip, supper and music cost five shillings a head.

INVASIVE PLANTS

Of concern to boaties, swimmers and anglers is the presence in Lake Wanaka of the introduced oxygen weed *Lagarosiphon major*. This invasive aquatic plant can form clogging swathes along the shoreline to depths of about six metres. It was recorded in the lake in 1973 and has since spread down the Clutha River to Lake Dunstan. Lake Hawea remains free of the weed so far, presumably because lake levels fluctuate so widely that the plant is unable to establish itself.

Lagarosiphon can re-establish from pieces as small as 2cm. Boat owners are therefore urged to clean their craft carefully on removal from any place infested with the weed, and to hose down and dry all equipment such as water skis, 'biscuits' or fishing gear.

Found exposed on parts of the shoreline is an introduced aquatic algae that produces a brown-green slime ('lake slime') in the right conditions. Probably of North American origin, it was discovered in Lake Wanaka in 2004 and now infests several South Island lakes. Research into control methods is ongoing. Boaties and anglers should make sure their boats and gear are clean after use.

GOING FISHING

Lakes Wanaka and Hawea and the rivers feeding them collectively enjoy an international reputation for fine angling. Trout were first released into Lake Wanaka in 1876 and Lake Hawea in 1911, and for many years a trout hatchery operated in Wanaka, resupplying the lakes with young fish.

From Wanaka you can walk, bike, boat or drive to many fishing spots. There is a fishing exclusion zone around the Wanaka waterfront protecting Bullock Creek, the hatchery stream. The zone arcs roughly from the marina across to Wanaka Station Park and includes the jetty by the information centre, where large trout often wait for visitors to feed them. All others parts of the shoreline are available to anglers. A 'fly only' restriction applies to the 1km stretch of the Upper Clutha River (north bank) known as Deans Bank. This zone starts at the first rapids below the outlet and extends almost to the Albert Town bridge.

A number of professional fishing guides operate out of Wanaka, some of whom have their own boats. You can also hire small boats for fishing.

Ask in sports shops for advice and tips on where and when to go fishing and what gear to use. The shops supply information on licences and local rules, and this is also available on the Fish & Game New Zealand website: www.fishandgame.org.nz.

TOP: Anglers on the Wilkin River give a tramper a lift.
ABOVE: Boating and fishing fun at Stevensons Arm.

ABOVE: Sky diving over Lake Wanaka.
SKYDIVE WANAKA

IN THE AIR

Adventure in the air takes a number of forms. From Wanaka Airport you can go on sightseeing flights over the nearby lakes and mountains and as far afield as Milford Sound and Aoraki/Mt Cook. Landings in remote places, where permitted, are possible for climbers, skiers and snowboarders, mountain bikers, trampers and hunters. Aerobatics in legendary aircraft such as a Tiger Moth or stunt planes can also be arranged.

If you prefer to fly without wings – at least for part of the experience – you can choose from skydiving, paragliding and parasailing.

RIGHT: Parasailing on Lake Wanaka.
WANAKA PARASAILING

OPPOSITE: A skier sends powder snow flying above the Cardrona base buildings. CARDRONA ALPINE RESORT
RIGHT: Skiers have grand views of Lake Wanaka on a clear day. TREBLE CONE SKI AND SNOWBOARD RESORT

ON THE SNOW SLOPES

Wanaka is a winter wonderland for snowsport enthusiasts. The ski season runs from June to October but varies according to snowfall. There are two downhill skiing and snowboarding fields – Cardrona and Treble Cone – relatively handy to town. Treble Cone is located in the Harris Mountains and Cardrona occupies an extension of the Crown Range. Across the valley from the Cardrona field is the Snow Farm (formerly Waiorau Snow Farm), which utilises the relatively level summit area of the Pisa Range for cross-country skiing and snowshoeing.

Treble Cone Ski Area is accessed off Mount Aspiring Road past Glendhu Bay (29km from town). The field covers 550ha (10 per cent rated for beginning skiers, 45 per cent intermediate, 45 per cent advanced), and runs from a base elevation of 1260m to a summit of 2088m.

Cardrona Alpine Resort is reached from Cardrona Valley Road (36km from town) and is located at 1669m. The field covers 345ha (25 per cent rated for beginners, 25 per cent intermediate, 30 per cent advanced and 20 per cent expert), and ranges from 1260 to 1860m elevation. Cardrona's skiing and snowboarding facilities allow it to host international competitions. Apartment accommodation is available.

The **Snow Farm** is also reached from Cardrona Valley Road (37km from town). The base, at about 1500m above sea level, offers lodge accommodation. Snowshoes and other gear can be rented, and activities are family-friendly. There are 55km of trails available.

All skifield access roads have a gravel surface, so chains should be carried and may need to be fitted on the drive to the skifield carpark. Ski gear, snowboards and chains can be hired from shops in town or from the skifield operators.

5

THE WILD SIDE

BIRD LIFE

From the opportunistic sparrows of downtown Wanaka to the clever and sometimes destructive kea (alpine parrots) of the Treble Cone carpark, and from the mistletoe-laden beech forest of Kidds Bush to the tussock grasslands on Mt Roy, the Wanaka region's flora and fauna are diverse and interesting.

Native bush birds such as grey warbler/riroriro, bellbird/korimako and South Island fantail/pīwakawaka are reasonably common in and around wooded areas of town. You will almost certainly encounter some of these species on the Mt Iron track or the lakefront walkways. The South Island tomtit/miromiro and brown creeper/pīpipi are less common.

Rangeland birds such as the New Zealand pipit/pīhoihoi and the introduced yellowhammer, green finch and goldfinch are likely to be seen at Rocky Mountain and sometimes on the Roys Peak track. The tail-flicking pipit, brown overall with white streaks, is similar in appearance to the introduced skylark, and has a habit of running ahead of trampers and flying out of the way if people come within a radius of about five metres.

Both of New Zealand's daytime birds of prey – the Australasian swamp harrier/kāhu, familiarly known as a hawk, and the less common New Zealand falcon/kārearea – are found in the Wanaka area. The harrier, which gets most of its food by scavenging, is commonly seen slowly patrolling farmland and highways, where roadkill of introduced rabbits, possums and hedgehogs provide good pickings. Slow

OPPOSITE: A kea inspects a stoat trap on a mountainside above the Matukituki River. CHRIS RILEY/ECO WANAKA ADVENTURES
RIGHT: Stoat traps are checked on a heli-hike adventure to mountains near Wanaka. ECO WANAKA ADVENTURES

down if you see a harrier feeding on roadkill as these birds are large and may not be able to lift off quickly enough to get out of your way.

Smaller, faster and more agile than the harrier, the New Zealand falcon is less often seen or recognised, but there are usually one or two reports of individuals flying over the town during the year. Falcons take only live prey, usually birds, which they chase through the air. In this region they generally nest on rock bluffs near water.

Like the falcon, the kea is also a threatened native species. These parrots, unusual because of their preference for mountain habitats, are found in some western areas of the Wanaka region close to high mountains. The Rob Roy Valley and Treble Cone skifield offer good opportunities for seeing them. Please do not feed kea. The practice makes them accustomed to human food and attracts them to places such as carparks, where they are liable to cause annoying damage to cars by tearing at the rubber on windows and wiper blades and the soft fittings on roof racks.

Two other birds at risk – the mohua/yellowhead and the rock wren – also inhabit the western mountains of the Wanaka region. Mohua, bright-yellow songsters of the forest, are sometimes seen in the upper Makarora Valley. For most visitors, however, the Blue Pools track north of Makarora provides probably the best opportunity of a sighting. Rock wrens – small, dainty and inconspicuous – are exclusively alpine birds and live above the treeline. Populations are known to inhabit upper parts of the West Matukituki Valley, and trampers and climbers sometimes encounter them around the Liverpool and French Ridge huts.

California quail, introduced in the 1860s, favour dry semi-open shrubland. They feed and socialise on the ground but will fly a short distance if alarmed. Drier lowland areas around Wanaka provide good habitat for these birds.

Among the native water birds, New Zealand scaup and paradise shelduck/pūtakitaki are common. The squat, dark scaup spends most of its time in the lakes, diving for food on the lakebed. You will often see them along the Wanaka lakefront, especially around the jetty, where they compete with the trout for food pellets thrown by visitors. Introduced mallard ducks and mallard/grey duck hybrids are the commonest ducks on the lake. They are the ones that will take food from picnickers and visitors strolling along the water's edge.

Two birds more commonly associated with the sea coast are prominent around Wanaka in certain seasons. Black-billed gulls are plentiful on the lakes and riverbeds in spring and summer, and smaller numbers of South Island pied oystercatcher/tōrea venture inland in late winter to breed on farmland or in the mountain ranges. The larger black-backed gull/kāroro is also seen in the wider Wanaka region at times.

CLOCKWISE FROM TOP LEFT: A female tomtit with a moth; South Island robins are often found on the forest floor; the New Zealand pipit inhabits grassy rangelands; a New Zealand pigeon grazes on plantain at Kidds Bush; a pair of New Zealand scaup at the Wanaka waterfront. The male has a bright yellow eye.

A gathering of grebes

Since 2014, a mission to help a threatened and little-known native bird, the Australasian crested grebe or pūteketeke, has been taking place at Wanaka marina. The birds, diving specialists that eat fish and aquatic invertebrates, prefer large glacial lakes and can stay submerged for up to a minute. The boat harbour has become a showcase breeding area for this rare and special species, of which only a few hundred remain in New Zealand.

It all started when Wanaka zoologist John Darby noticed that the nests of a number of grebes were failing because of fluctuating lake levels. Grebes generally build a floating nest in shoreline vegetation, but this will fail if the nest is flooded or if water levels drop, leaving it high and dry.

With assistance from Mount Aspiring College, Darby designed and built floating platforms that would rise and fall on the marina piles. The grebes immediately took advantage of these, creating cosy nests from vegetation that Darby and his volunteer group supplied or that the birds themselves collected. Word spread on the grebe grapevine, and by the summer of 2017–18 grebes in the marina had produced more than 200 chicks from up to 40 nests. Some pairs even began nesting in mid-winter – a breeding behaviour not previously recorded. In summer the marina is busy with motorboats, but that does not deter the grebes. They seem to know their homes are protected from human disturbance, predators and dogs.

The grebes have become a Wanaka icon, attracting bird watchers from around New Zealand and overseas. The footpath above the marina is a perfect grandstand for observing their extraordinary courtship dances, territorial disputes and their endearing practice of carrying chicks on their backs. Regular newspaper columns written by Darby keep the locals informed of breeding success.

BUFF WEKA HOMECOMING

The reintroduction of buff weka to the Wanaka area is a wildlife project with a difference. The birds originally inhabited the South Island east of the Main Divide and had become extinct in Central Otago in the 1920s, but a population survived in the Chathams. Thirty buff weka chicks were initially transferred from the Chatham Islands to Stevensons Island/Te Peka Karara in 2002, through a joint project by Otago iwi (Kāi Tahu Papatipu Rūnaka o Ōtākou) and the Department of Conservation, with the cooperation of the Chatham Islands people.

Initially the weka were free-ranging on Stevensons Island. Being good swimmers, some escaped to the mainland – and predators like stoats were able to swim to the island. All remaining birds were eventually transferred to predator-free Mou Waho and two islands on Lake Wakatipu.

A buff weka on Mou Waho checks out a potted cabbage tree seedling that will contribute to the island's revegetation. ECO WANAKA ADVENTURES

CLOCKWISE FROM TOP LEFT: A native tree daisy, *Olearia macrodonta*, produces clusters of honey-scented flowers; the scarlet flowers of a native mistletoe in beech forest at Kidds Bush; native jasmine flowering on a marbleleaf tree at Kidds Bush; a native aniseed, *Gingidia montana*, in the Rob Roy Valley; Wahlenbergia, a native alpine flower, in the upper Rob Roy Valley.

PLANT LIFE

Vegetation patterns vary according to exposure to wet and dry conditions, winter snow and ice, summer heat and altitude. East of the two big lakes, grassland and shrubland prevail in the 'rainshadow' of the Main Divide mountains. Patches of beech forest cling to a few mountain valleys, reminders of a time when beech and podocarp forest was much more widely distributed throughout the region. These remnant patches are mainly mountain beech, the species most tolerant of dry conditions. Kidds Bush, on the wetter, western side of Lake Hawea, has a substantial mountain beech forest, with an understorey of kōhūhū, wineberry, marbleleaf and tree fuchsia. North of Makarora, silver beech predominates, and a good example of this can be seen on the Blue Pools track.

Majestic red beech forest, Glacier Burn, East Matukituki.

West of the lakes, higher rainfall spilling over the Main Divide encourages more extensive forest growth. Beech dominates the canopy, with silver beech the main species. The larger-leafed red beech, a handsome tree reaching about 30m in height, favours warmer sites. There are impressive stands of red beech near Aspiring Hut in the West Matukituki Valley and at Glacier Burn in the East Matukituki.

Bracken fern swathes the lower slopes of many mountains in the Wanaka region. A native plant, it is a rapid coloniser of disturbed areas and has profited from fires in the past.

Two rare plant species – a shrub and a small tree – are the subject of conservation efforts. *Hebe cuppressoides*, a rounded bush with tight foliage and small mauve flowers, is found in the Lake Hawea area. *Olearia hectori*, a member of the tree daisy family, occurs on river flats in the

Matagouri shrubs and tussock grasses dominate the vegetation on this glaciated landscape around Rocky Mountain in the Matukituki Valley.

TOP: The McCanns skink is found up to an altitude of 1500m. IAN SOUTHEY
ABOVE: This species of mountain wētā, a large insect, lives on the island of Mou Waho.

Matukituki Valley, and plantings of it can be seen around Raspberry Creek car park.

LIZARDS

The Wanaka region generally, and the islands of Lake Wanaka in particular, harbour good populations of both skinks and geckos. The most commonly encountered is McCanns skink, which is dark brown with lighter stripes. It is found throughout the Central Otago valleys and on mountains to an altitude of about 1500m.

The endangered Otago skink, glossy black with gold splotches and the largest skink species of all, is restricted to a small area near Hawea.

Skinks have shiny tight skins and narrow heads and are usually active during the day; geckos are more active around dusk, their skin is dull and velvety, their heads are flatter and their eyes more conspicuous. Distributions of the Southern Alps and Cromwell Gorge geckos overlap around Wanaka. The Southern Alps gecko, large and stocky, is adapted to live at higher altitudes.

WĒTĀ

Among the diverse array of insects inhabiting the Wanaka region, the flightless wētā is eye-catching. The islands of Mou Waho and Mou Tapu have significant populations of the large wētā *Hemideina maori*. Curiously, it is found elsewhere in Otago only on mountain ranges or at much higher altitudes than the Wanaka islands.

MOUNT ASPIRING NATIONAL PARK

Wanaka's western wilderness, Mount Aspiring National Park, straddles a backbone of glaciated mountains – the southernmost sector of the Southern Alps. It extends from the Haast Pass area in the north to the Humboldt Mountains near the head of Lake Wakatipu. Since it was created in 1964 the park has almost doubled in size through the addition of various parcels of land and, after Fiordland and Kahurangi in Northwest Nelson, it is now New Zealand's third-largest national park. Wanaka

TOP: Tititea/Mt Aspiring viewed from the Cascade Saddle area. LEFT: Beech forest and Rob Roy Glacier.

is the main gateway to it, with Mount Aspiring Road a spectacular entrance to the geographical centre of the park via the Matukituki Valley.

The park's character, embracing icy summits, vast snowfields, sheer rock bluffs, forested gorges and pleasant river flats, has long enchanted artists and lured trampers, climbers and adventurers. Within the park's boundaries lie some of mainland New Zealand's most wild and remote areas. About 20 per cent of the total area of the park is officially designated wilderness, where there are no tracks, bridges or huts. The upper reaches of valleys extending east from the Main Divide have been incorporated into the park, with cattle and sheep farms adjoining the boundaries.

Over the years visitor use has increased as a result of the construction of short walks and longer tramping tracks, and with the advent of commercial ventures such as jetboat tours, helicopter flights and guided fishing, hunting and climbing trips. Only one road crosses from east to west – the Haast Pass highway.

The park takes its name from southern New Zealand's pre-eminent peak, New Zealand's highest mountain outside the Mt Cook region. Tititea/Mt Aspiring is a glacial horn that has been sculpted back to a pinnacle by successive glaciations. From the west it appears as a New Zealand 'Matterhorn', but from the Wanaka area it has a blunter profile.

The Department of Conservation's Wanaka visitor centre has an exhibit about the national park, and other displays can be viewed at the department's Makarora, Haast and Queenstown visitor centres.

FURTHER READING

Brodie, Ian and Philip Makaana, *The Best of Warbirds Over Wanaka*, Auckland: Penguin, 2002.

Irvine, Roxburgh, *Wanaka and Surrounding Districts*, Upper Clutha 1990 Community Committee, 1990.

Peat, Neville and Brian Patrick, *Wild Central: Exploring the natural history of Central Otago*, Dunedin: University of Otago Press, 1999.

Van Reenen, Gilbert, *The Nature of Wanaka*, Wanaka: Clean Green Press, 2012.

The author on a cycle trail.

INDEX

Bold page numbers indicate illustrations

A

Aeolus, Mt/Oblong Peak 19
Albert Town 4, 12, 16, 17, **17**, 19, 33 20, **34**, 35, **39**, 43, 44, 53, 54, 61; Bridge 20, 33, 35, 61
Alpine club 50
Alta, Mt 12, 15, 54
Anderson Road 43
Aoraki/Mt Cook 19, 37, 62, 77
Arethusa Pool 11, 21, **59**, 59
Aspiring, Mt/Tititea 4, 7, 11, 15, 19, 28, 36, **40**, 41, 44, 46, 48, 49, 54, **54**, **76**, 77; College 70; Hut 50, 54, 73; Road 29, 54, 64, 77
Aubrey Road 32, 43

B

Beacon Point 13, 42
bellbird/korimako 43, 67
biking/cycling 39, 42, 53, 54
birds **11**, 14, 44, 48, 53, 67, 68, 70, 71
black-backed gull/kāroro 68
Black Peak 15, 54
Blue Pools 52, **53**, 68, 73
Bremner Bay 42
brown creeper/pīpipi 44, 53, 67
Buchanan Peaks **12**, 54
Bull Islet 60

C

cabbage tree/tī kōuka 14, **20**, 59, **71**
campsites 33, **33**; Albert Town 35, 54; campervans **13**; camping 30, 32, 35, 59; Kidds Bush 33, 51; Māori 14
canoe 13, 14, 43 57, **57**, 60
canyon 57
Cardrona 4, 35, 7; Hotel **34**, 35; Alpine Resort (ski field) 35, 54, **64**, 65; Distillery 34, 35; Folk Festival 28, 30; Valley 16, 17, 44, 46
Chalmers Street Lookout 19, 25
Chalmers, Nathanael 19
cinema 30
climbing **25**, 30, 31, 54, **54**, 77; climbing wall **24**, 30, 31
Clutha River/Matu Au 12, **16**, 17, 19, 20, 33, 34, 35, **37**, 39, **39**, 42, **42**, 43, 53, 57, 60, 61; Clutha Valley 7, 44
Colquhouns Beach 50
Cook, Mt/Aoraki 19, 37, 62, 77
coprosma **48**
cycling/biking 39, 42, 53, 54

D

Damper Bay 44, 45
Darby, John 4, 70, 71
Diamond Lake 7, 46, **47**, 47, 48; Track 47, **48**

E

Eely Point 42, **42**

F

falcon/kārearea 50, 67, 68
fantail/pīwakawaka 43, 53, 67
fly-fishing 28, 43
French Ridge hut 68
Fuchsia excorticata/tree fuchsia/ kōtukutuku 47, 47, 51, 73

G

gecko 75
gold miners 17
goldfields 17, 57
Grandview Mountain **5**, 19
grebe, Australasian crested/ pūteketeke 70, 71, **70**
grey duck/pārera 14, 68
grey warbler/riroriro 43, 53, 67

H

hapū, Ngāti Hāwea 14
Harris Mountains 7, 46, 48, 54, 64
Harwich Island/Mou Waho 11, 58, 71, **71**, **75**, 75
Hawea 14, 27, 51, 75; Flat 19, 46; Glacier 7; Hāwea, Ngati 14; Holiday Park 33; River 7, 20, 33, 35, 54, 57
Hawea, Lake 4, 7, 12, 14, **14**, **16**, 19, **20**, 20, **21**, 33, 36, 39, 44,

46, 51, 52, 54, 59, 60, 61, 73;
    boating guide 57
holiday parks 32, 33, 42, 43
hydroelectric 20, 37

I

Iron, Mt 15, 19, 31, **43**, 44, **60**;
    Track 67
Ironside Hill **15**, 44, 45

J

jetboat 57, 77

K

kāhu/Australasian swamp
    harrier 67, 68
Kāi Tahu Papatipu Rūnaka 71
kākāpō 14
kānuka 44
kārearea/falcon 50, 67
kāroro/black-backed gull 68
kayak 43, 57, 60
Kidds Bush 10, 14, **14**, **33**, 33, 51,
    51, 52, 67, **69**, **72**, 73; campsite
    33
kererū/pigeon, New Zealand 14,
    43, **69**
kō/digging stick 14
kōhūhū 51, 73
kōnini 47
koreke/quail 14
korimako/bellbird 43, 67
kōtukutuku/tree fuchsia/*Fuchsia
    excorticata* **47**, 47, 51, 73
kōwhai **14**, 42, 59

L

lemonwood 51
Liverpool Huts 68
lizards 75
log rafts 57

M

Main Divide 22, **22**, 71, 73, 77
Makarora 7, 10, 20, 33, 36, 47,
    51, 52, 57, 73; Bush 52; camp
    ground 52; motor camp 37;
    River 52; Valley 7, 17, 53, 68;
    Visitor Centre 4, 52, 77; walks
    52
mānuka 42, 43, 44, 59
Manuka Island/Pigeon Island 58
marbleleaf 51, **51**, **72**, 73
Matu Au/Clutha River 12, **16**, 17,
    19, 20, 33, 34, 35, **37**, 39, **39**,
    42, **42**, 43, 53, 57, 60, 61
Matukituki **73**; River 7, **7**, **15**,
    22, **33**, 48, **48**, 49, **49**, **50**, **66**;
    Valley 7, 14, 17, 46, 50, 54, **55**,
    68, **74**, 75, 77
McKerrow Range **21**, 51
Millennium Track 15, 44, **45**,
    45, **60**
Minaret Burn 50, **50**, **40**; Peaks 54
miromiro/tomtit 67, **69**

mistletoe, native **14**, 51, 67, **72**
mohua/yellowhead 53, 68
motor camp 32; Glendhu Bay 32,
    45; Makarora 37
Mou Tapu **6**, 48, 58, **58**, 59, 75
Mou Waho/Harwich Island 11,
    21, 48, 57, 58, **59**, 59, 71, **71**,
    75
mountain-bike track 45, 53, 54

Mountain Film and Book
    Festival 28
Mt Cook/Aoraki 19, 37, 62, 77

N

National Park 37, 50; Mt
    Aspiring 4, 11, 49, 54, 76, 77;
    Mt Cook 19
Neck, the **10**, 14, 20, **21**, 36, 51, **59**
Ngāti Hāwea 14

O

Oanaka/Wanaka 4, 5, 6, 7, 10, 11,
    12, 13, 14, 15, 16, **18**, 19, 20,
    22, 24, **25**, **26**, 27, 28, 29, 31,
    31, 32, 35, 36, 37, 39, **40**, 42,
    44, 46, 49, 52, 53, 54, 57, 61,
    64, 67, 68, 71, 77
Oblong Peak/Mt Aeolus 19
Outlet Road 42, 43

P

paradise shelduck/pūtakitaki 68
pārera/grey duck 14
Pembroke **16**, **17**, **18**, 19
Pembroke Park 13, 16, 37
Penrith Beach 42
pied oystercatcher/tōrea 68
    pigeon, New Zealand/
    kererū 14, 43, **69**
Pigeon Island/Manuka Island 58
pīhoihoi/pipit 48, 67, **69**
pīpipi/brown creeper 44, 53, 67
pipit/pīhoihoi 48, 67, **69**
pīwakawaka/fantail 67, 43, 53
pūtakitaki/paradise shelduck 68
pūteketeke/Australasian crested
    grebe 70
Puzzling World 31, **31**, 44

Q

quail/koreke 14; California quail
    68
Queenstown 4, 11, 12, 28, 77

R

raft 57; historical 17, 19
Rākaihautū 14
Raspberry Creek 49, 54; carpark
    50, 75
raupō 19
riroriro/grey warbler 43, 53, 67
riverboard/sledge 57
Rob Roy Glacier **49**, 50, **76**

Rob Roy Valley 49, **49**, 68, **72**;
    stream 49, **49**
Rocky Mountain 9, **33**, 46, 48, **48**.
    67, **74**
Roy, Mt **47**, 67
Roys Bay 7, 8, **10**, **11**, **12**, **13**, 13,
    16, **17**, 19, 28, 42, 43, 57, **57**,
    59; Recreation Reserve 37
Roys Peak 15, **38**, 46, **47**; track
    33, 67
Ruby Island 43, 44, 58, **60**, 60

S
Salix fragilis (crack willow) **8**
Sawyer Burn 52
skink 75, **75**
Skyline Track 46
sledge/riverboard 57
Snow Farm 64
snowberry flowers **48**
Southern Alps 7, 8, 10, 22, 44, 45,
    50, 75, 76
Spotts Creek 46
Stevensons Arm 19, 59, 61
Stevensons Island/Te Peka
    Karara 58, 59, 60, 71
swamp harrier, Australasian/
    kāhu 67, 68
swing bridge **49**, 49, 52

T
Te Peka Karara/Stevensons
    Island 58, 59, 60, 71
Thomson, John Turnbull 16, 19
tī kōuka/cabbage tree **20**
Timaru Creek 20
Tititea/Mt Aspiring 4, 7, 11, 15,
    19, 28, 36, **40**, 41, 44, 46, 48,
    49, 54, **54**, **76**, 77
tomtit/miromiro 67, **69**
tōrea/pied oystercatcher 68
trampers **6**, 11, 46, 50, 62, 67,
    68, 77
Treble Cone 15, 48, 54, 65, **65**, 68;
    carpark 67
Tuohys Lagoon **36**

U
Upper Clutha Agricultural and
    Pastoral Show 27
Upper Clutha Messenger 36
uruao (ocean-going canoe or
    waka) 14

W
waka 14
Wanaka/Oanaka Airport 62;
    artisan market 27; Beerworks
    31; Challenge 27; cinemas 30;
    holiday programme 27; Hotel
    18; islands 10, 48, 58, **58**, 59
    75; Library 30 Millennium
    Track 15, 44, **45**, **60**; pool 30;
    rodeo 27; Station Park 16, 17,
    43, 44, 61; Transport and Toy
    Museum 31; Visitor Centre 4,
    52, 77
Wanaka, Lake 7, 8, 12, 14, 16, 17,
    19, 20, **21**, 22, **22**, 30, 32, 33,
    36, 37, 39, 48, **48**, **50**, **58**, 59,
    60, 61, **62**, **63**, 68, **69**; boating
    guide 57; centre 27, 30;
    marina **11**, 70
Wanaka tree **8**
Warbirds over Wanaka 28, 29, **29**,
    31, 77
water activities 57
water skis 60
Waterfall Creek 4, 15, 43, 44, 45,
    60, **60**
weka 14, 59, 71, **71**
West Wanaka Road 50
West Wanaka Station 50
wētā 75, **75**
whisky 35
Wilkin River 57, **61**
Wilkin, Robert 44
willow 43; *Salix fragilis* (crack
    willow) **8**
wineberry 51, 73
Winter Games 28

Y
yellowhead/mohua 54, 68